Who Would You Be If...

How to reclaim your life and become a happy,
authentic and stress-free woman

PATRICIA FITZGERALD

RED STAG

First published in 2018 by
Red Stag
An imprint of Mentor Books
43 Furze Road, Sandyford Industrial Estate,
Dublin 18, Ireland

Tel. +353 1 295 2112/3   Fax. +353 1 295 2114
email: admin@mentorbooks.ie
www.mentorbooks.ie

ISBN: 978-1-912514-27-4

A catalogue record for this book is available
from the British Library.

Cover Design: Anú Design
Editing, design and layout: Nicola Sedgwick
Labyrinth and mandala images: Patricia Fitzgerald

Printed in Ireland

1 3 5 7 9 8 6 4 2

For Rebecca

Contents

Acknowledgements

I would like to extend a massive thank you to the people who have helped and supported me in writing this book. Firstly, to the late Danny McCarthy of Mentor Books, with whom I had initial meetings about the project. Danny was such a beautiful person, a gentle, supportive and enthusiastic soul whose presence is sorely missed by many. Ar dheis Dé go raibh a anam.

Thank you to Declan Collinge, poet and commissioning editor at Mentor Books, who read my mandala art blogs and approached me about writing the book. Thank you for believing in me. Deep gratitude to Nicola Sedgwick, my wonderful editor. Nicola has been a pleasure to work with and showed such patience and support, even when I kept mixing up when to use the word 'practice' or 'practise'. Some day that will click! Thank you, Nicola, for everything. Thank you to Daniel McCarthy and everyone at Mentor Books for all their work and support. Thanks to Anú Design for the wonderful job they did on the book cover.

Thanks to Brian O'Gabhain (Áras Chrónáin), Alan McGrath (sound technician) and Tony Mohan of Mid Atlantic for the work on creating the meditation CD. Thanks to Ian Morris of Listening To Smile, Vermont, USA for the license to use the wonderfully healing music in the meditations. A massive thanks for the support and mentorship of Tara Prendergast of Bite the Biscuit online creative community. Thanks to all the factory biccies . . . you know who you are!

Thanks to Clare Lennon, Amanda Grace, Emer Halpenny and Caitríona Breathnach for all the support and chats. Thanks to the wonderful Sophias: Donna Redmond, Fiona Smith, Adele Smiddy and Finola McFadden for the enlightening chats and beautiful friendship. Thank you to all the people who have attended my workshops. I always love these gatherings and learn so much from each and every person who comes.

And last but not least, thanks to my family, especially Conor Graham and my splendiferous daughter Rebecca and her sidekick Boo Radley, who teach me so much every day.

Introduction

Who would you be if you weren't weighed down by challenges, obstacles and negative situations? You will find out as you read this book and apply the knowledge therein to your own life.

In our society women have often been conditioned to keep small. To be the good girl. Not to be too pushy. To always be polite. To be pretty. To be the perfect mother. The perfect wife. The perfect daughter. So much so that we often give ourselves completely away. We drain away our energy and our dreams go down the plughole too. Because that's what good girls do, right? We often become too drained to be of any good to anyone. We can become resentful or perhaps even bitter that we cannot fulfil our potential.

For a woman, caring for herself, developing herself or doing things for herself has in the past been considered selfish. 'Selfish' is not a very nice word. How about we change that to 'self full'? What would it be like if you became full of your authentic self? Doing the things you love to do. Being the woman you were always meant to be.

When we step into our power as women and live the life that we deeply desire, we become so much happier in ourselves. We are so much more fulfilled. And then we naturally become good mothers, daughters, sisters, wives, partners, friends. It's not hard work any more. We are coming to it from a different place with a different energy. We are empowered, honest and authentic. When we give, we are no longer drained or resentful; instead we are filled up. We are in tune with our deepest and truest selves.

The book is written in a particular order and sequence. Each chapter builds on the one before, and it is important for you to learn, work on and integrate the information and exercises before progressing onwards. And of course your progress will not be linear; that's not how life works! It will be more like a labyrinth. As a visual example, trace the labyrinth below with your finger.

You can see how the path meanders back and forth before you reach the centre. As you develop, you will recognise these times as opportunities to revisit and clear out certain fears, obstacles or negative thinking that are lurking in your subconscious mind. Then you can resume your journey towards authenticity and transformation with ever-greater clarity and purpose.

- In **Chapter One** I share a little of my own journey and how I have come to be doing this work, and indeed writing this book. You will also learn about your personal guidance system.

- In **Chapter Two** you take a deep look inside yourself to acknowledge where you are right now and become clear on where you wish to go. Getting to know yourself is key: if you don't know where you are and where you want to go, you can never get there!

- In **Chapter Three** we cover general mindfulness practices. Becoming present is a gift to yourself and the more moments you can practise presence, the more powerful it will be in your life. Being in the moment and appreciating it will allow you to experience more ease in life, and this will compliment the work that you will do in this book.

- In **Chapter Four** we take a look at our relationship with time. Worrying about time can be a distraction for many of us and the concept of 'not having enough time' can often be an excuse not to move ahead.

- Personal growth and moving towards your dreams requires you to overcome fears that you may hold both consciously and unconsciously. In **Chapter Five**, we look fear straight in the face…

literally! We walk right up to it, hands on hips, and we talk to it, argue with it and get to know it well.

- In **Chapter Six** we deal with different ways of building up your resilience. This skill is necessary on your journey to finding your authentic self. Resilience is something that some people seem to have been born with, while for others, it is something that must be learned.

- **Chapter Seven** offers you ways of dealing with negative thinking. You will discover how to avoid automatically jumping into negative thoughts or scenarios and will instead learn how to default to positive thinking. We also look at uncovering limiting beliefs that may be holding you back. Unearthing and reframing these beliefs is a powerful practice in helping you move forward.

- In **Chapter Eight**, we look at gratitude practices. Gratitude is a skill we can profit from enormously. Being grateful is the opposite of being discontented, and gratitude will boost your resilience and increase your positivity. You will become happier, and this clearer energy will move you towards better decision-making and creative thoughts and ideas.

- The act of forgiving both others and yourself holds great power. In **Chapter Nine** you will see how forgiveness frees you from resentment and gives you peace of mind. The Buddha compared holding onto anger to grasping a hot coal with the intent of throwing it at someone else. You, of course, are the one who gets burned. Letting go of the hot coals will help you create the peaceful and successful life that you desire.

- In **Chapter Ten**, we move our attention towards creative visualisation. You will have gained clarity by now on where you are at the moment and where you want to go. You will explore ways of manifesting your desired future self by creating a vision board and by creative visualisation meditation. These methods seed your intentions deep into your subconscious mind and with practice you will find ideas and opportunities coming to you more quickly and easily.

- **Chapter Eleven** looks at the art of self-care. What you are doing in this book is deep and courageous work, and it is vital to look after yourself well in mind, body and spirit. This final chapter provides you with many self-care routines you can choose from that will suit your own particular lifestyle.

I have personally found meditation to be a profound tool on the path of personal development. To accompany this book, I have created several guided meditations specifically designed to deepen the work you will be doing. See pp. 149-151 for more details. For a small fee you can access them at www.healingcreations.ie, where they are available as CDs or as digital downloads.

Please note: It is not mandatory to purchase the meditations to benefit from the content and exercises provided in this book.

May you enjoy each step of your amazing journey towards happiness, fulfilment and peace of mind.

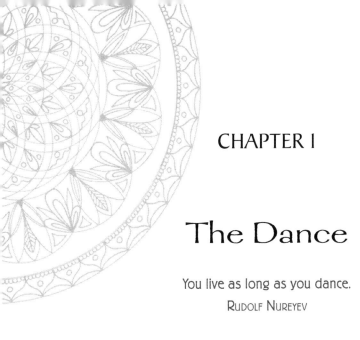

CHAPTER 1

The Dance

You live as long as you dance.
RUDOLF NUREYEV

Change can be difficult. Oftentimes we are not quite sure what needs to change, only that some 'thing' does. You may feel it is something external, for example, a relationship, a job or a home. Or maybe it is something internal. You could be experiencing an uneasy feeling of 'Is this it?', a deep-rooted knowing that you are not living to your true potential and that there is something more you want to do and be in the world. In my experience, all change begins inside us. When we master our mind and spirit, and become clear on what we really want and where we want to go, then the external situations change and transform with much greater ease.

When we want to change something, we have to be brutally honest with ourselves. We need to dig deep and be prepared to get the shovel dirty. Are you willing to take a good look inside and out?

I once had a friend who paid to go to a mindfulness course as she felt she was stressed and constantly ruminating. The group met once a week for two hours. She was on week four and I asked her how she was getting on. She said, 'I think it's a bit rubbish. I feel good for a few hours after, but then it's back to normal. It's not having any real effect, and I'm still as stressed out as ever.' I asked her what kind of things they talked about. She told me. I asked was she practicing them? 'No, not really, I suppose,' was her reply. She also added, 'But I've been going to the course for four weeks now, and I expected things to change.'

Making the effort to change
Reading the books, watching the videos, or showing up at a course is great. This means there is definitely something in your life you want to change. That in itself is a huge acknowledgement not to be underestimated. The next step is to implement personal development practices into your own life. What you read here, or find on any personal development course or video, will not be absorbed by osmosis. I don't like to be the bearer of bad news, but that is a fact. Action is required, and deep down you know it.

The good news is that there is no wrong way to do this. You read this book. You take from it what feels right for you and your personality and your life as it stands. We are all unique. We all have different challenges and successes, and different balances of chemicals running through our brains and bodies.

Start with just one or two things that resonate. Practise those for a few weeks and then come back and take one or two more practices. Slow and steady wins the race. This is about getting to know yourself, forming new habits and breaking old ones that no longer serve you. Trying to do it all at once will only see you give up after a few days. Does that remind you of diets you tried, or attempts at getting fit?

What you will be doing now is accessing a voice of self-compassion within your mind instead of the voice of a default critic. It is gifting yourself the ability to move forward in your own time and become the creator of your life, rather than a passive bystander allowing life to happen to you.

Freeing your mind

I recently attended a mindfulness conference where I was one of a group of speakers. Someone in the audience asked for a description, in one sentence, of what mindfulness and personal development meant to each of us. I had a few moments to mull this over as other speakers went ahead of me. My reply was, 'It has released me from the prison of my own mind.' I didn't have much time to think of this line, but funnily, even if I had, I couldn't have come up with a better analogy.

Since beginning mindful practices, meditation and personal development in my own life, I find I have so much more time to do the things that I love. I am also calmer, there is less drama, I worry way less, and my inner voice is much kinder towards myself and others. So when that critical voice starts up, and it still does at times, I can catch it more easily and say, 'Thanks for your input, but not now, darling!'

That's a big win in anyone's book. I spent so much of my life worrying over small things, playing out in my mind negative scenarios that never actually happened. I also created stories and made amazing excuses for why I could not do a particular thing or pursue my dreams. I wasted so much energy. But you know what? When I look back on that way of being I can reverse think it. I acknowledge that I created great fiction in these incredible but horrific stories, and I had enough energy to worry a lot. The overall realisation was that I was simply using these two forces of creation and energy the wrong way.

Do you find yourself doing that? Think of the last time a problem or conflict arose. We often even do it with positive things, like a first date. Instead of wondering what will go right, we come up with a myriad of ways it could all go wrong. We are master storytellers. Have you fallen into a spiral of negative self-talk, imagining all the things that could go wrong, or all the things that you could have said to people if only you were a smarter person? We all do it.

> Say to yourself right now: 'I am filled with creative energy. I choose to create the life I want.'

You are a creator and that is a powerful thing. Now you can turn that creative energy around to your favour and benefit. And believe me, if I can do it, you absolutely can too. Say to yourself right now: 'I am filled with creative energy. I choose to create the life I want.'

How I began my journey

Let me tell you a little of how I stumbled upon mindfulness and personal development. In December 2012, I was not sleeping. I was stressed out, losing my temper and basically worrying all day. I was in the midst of massive and unexpected changes in my life. I was divorcing, the family home was up for sale and I did not know what was going to happen next. I wanted to control it all and simply could not. My life was not at all going as planned. I couldn't sleep at night because my brain kept whirring with horrendous scenarios and I ended up having to take sleeping tablets. I also had a pain in my jaw from clenching my teeth. It wasn't a pretty way of being.

At the time, my daughter was seven years old. She needed me and I was not present. My heart sank when I realised this. I knew that even though I tried to hide my worries from her, I still wasn't being the mother that she needed. And she especially needed me now. 'Mum, you're not listening!' she said to me one day. Children are perceptive, so much more than we think. And she was right – I wasn't listening. I hadn't heard the question she had asked and only became aware when she grabbed my attention. From then on, I became more alert and could see in her eyes her disappointment when I was not present and listening to her properly.

So I made a decision. I decided to spend quality time with her, during which I would be completely present. I chose our story time at bedtime, which I had up to then been racing through in order to go downstairs and worry some more in peace! Ironic, huh? But I made that decision.

Day one was difficult. My mind was wandering and I felt impatient. I persisted, even if my attempts at being in the moment were nearly a pretence. Day two, the same. On it went for a week or two. But gradually something magical happened. I began to actually be present, to become involved in the words of the story I was reading, to hear my voice and the story it told. I could look at my daughter and see all her beauty and innocence.

It was such a gift to both of us. I ended up looking forward to our time together each and every night during that stressful period. I had such gratitude for that shift in thinking, and before long I could feel the benefits. My jaw relaxed. I was able to crack a smile naturally and slowly, with baby steps, I began to bring this mindful practice into other areas of my time with my daughter: eating together, playing together, being present when I asked her about her day at school. I was really listening.

As I did this, I learned how to be present in other areas. I also relinquished control and worry in areas where I didn't have any control. I would do the actions physically required to make a situation better and then accept that there were parts that I simply couldn't do anything about, no matter what amount of worrying I was doing. Often we worry because it makes us feel that we are actually doing something constructive – even if that thing is worrying. I began to move through my fears.

I became present and calm in traffic, in my workplace, in line at the grocery store, and many other places. I changed my attitude and everything around me changed. Me standing in line tapping my foot and performing a litany of inner curses about the old lady rummaging for change at the till and holding up the queue was not going to change the fact that the queue was slow. I learned to accept. Okay, the line was moving slowly. What to do? Look around. I could smile at the person behind or ahead, start a chat. Then I could watch the whole energy of that queue change from one of stress to lightness. The old lady didn't sense animosity behind her any more and so she was able to find the change she needed more easily. The worker at the checkout was not getting a knot of stress in his or her stomach knowing that the line was extending moment by moment. I could see right in front of my eyes how positive energy spreads like a smile spreads from person to person.

> Positive energy spreads like a smile spreads from person to person.

Please be aware that negative energy spreads in the very same way. So which would you prefer? Because you absolutely have a choice.

As I embarked on this journey, I grew to know myself more and more: what dreams I had pushed beneath the surface, what I wanted to be in the world, how I wanted to feel in my life. Through much self-enquiry and through implementing personal development practices, I began changing bit by bit almost every part of my life. I have since moved from a job I had begun to hate to becoming a successful artist, author, teacher and meditation facilitator. I have enjoyed every moment of travelling along this path – and you can too. I moved through the fear of being alone, fear of what others might think, fear of not having a stable pay cheque, fear of stepping out of my comfort zone, fear of public speaking . . . and so much more! Eventually I discovered that freedom most definitely lies at the other side of fear. And as you work through challenges and realise this for yourself, each fear becomes a little easier to conquer.

Another thing I found was that my physical environment means a lot to me; it has a profound effect on the way I feel. Before I started working on myself, I hadn't been aware of quite how much this affected me. Now I find myself increasingly in the most beautiful places surrounded by nature and by supportive and interesting people who expand me. I could not have known these things or have got to this place in my life had I not undertaken a very deep questioning of myself, of what it is that truly makes me tick. What truly makes me happy.

There is one thing you need to acknowledge and deeply realise within yourself. Know that you are already enough and recognise the great job you have done so far in life. I know I had done the best in my life up to that point. However, something deep inside me knew that there was more that I could do, so I made a conscious choice to embark on this journey of personal development. There is nothing wrong with you as you are, right now in this moment. You simply feel the desire to move forward. Affirm that to yourself now. 'I am enough as I am. I choose to move forward because I want to.'

Your internal guidance system

Getting to know yourself is paramount. You need to know where you are starting from and where you want to go. You figure this out through deep self-enquiry. You have inside you a profound intuition or internal guidance system, almost like a GPS in a car. Something in this guidance system has urged you to buy this book and begin this journey.

We all have this inner knowing that nudges us deep inside when change is wanted or needed, even though we might not yet have a clear picture of where it wants us to go. To get to your destination, you need to key in clear information to your internal GPS. It will be your best friend on this journey and you will begin to trust it more and interact with it more frequently.

As you begin your personal development work you will begin to move in the direction of your dreams. Your internal guidance system will kick in more fully and will be there to help you. As you get to each place or goal more destinations will appear along the route. Momentum will increase as you travel towards your path to authenticity, the journey itself being the most enjoyable part. The journey is life.

Your goals will become almost secondary. Think of it like a dance. You might concentrate on correctly completing a beautiful dance at a certain point on the dance floor. But the finishing point isn't what the dance is about. It is about the graceful journey and movement to that part of the floor. The weaving, the circling, moving in and out. As you progress on your journey you will take steps forward, you will take

WHO WOULD YOU BE IF . . .

steps back. That is what is beautiful. That is what is magical. That is the dance of moving towards your authentic life.

Summary

- To change, you must be prepared to take action.

- The good news is that there is no wrong way to do this.

- Start with just one or two things that resonate.

- Have you fallen into a spiral of negative self-talk, imagining all the things that could go wrong?

- You are a creator and that is a powerful thing.

- Freedom lies on the other side of fear.

- Acknowledge the great job you have done so far in life.

- You have inside you a deep intuition or internal guidance system.

- Momentum will increase as you travel towards your path to authenticity, the journey itself being the most enjoyable part.

CHAPTER 2

Getting to Know You

Knowing others is wisdom; knowing yourself is enlightenment.

Lao Tzu

To begin this work, it is important to take a look at where you are at now, to really delve inside and find what makes you tick and what doesn't. What do you want to change? You may be conscious of what it is, or it may be something buried deeper within that you can't quite put your finger on. You may have a dream you want to fulfil, but aren't quite clear about it or where you want to go with it.

The questions on pages 28-29 are aimed at getting to know yourself at the core of you. You may have already achieved some success in doing what you love, but that may have been by sheer luck. However, if you do the work and completely focus on looking inside, you will be able to move forward in a more effective way. Think about it: when you want to get to know someone, you do that by spending time with them, by talking with them and by asking questions about themselves. Some of the revelations you uncover during self-inquiry may be a complete surprise, so simply allow yourself to be open to whatever comes up.

The questionnaire is a brilliant exercise to do once or twice a year. It will give you a starting point for living in alignment with who you truly are. No longer will you operate by accident or luck, but rather on purpose, by intention, by design. You will know yourself more fully and where it is that you want to go. And when you know yourself better you can also become more compassionate towards yourself. You can become your own best friend and offer yourself good and valuable advice! You can trust yourself.

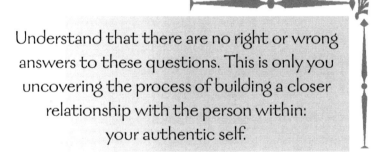

Understand that there are no right or wrong answers to these questions. This is only you uncovering the process of building a closer relationship with the person within: your authentic self.

Schedule blocks of time to interview yourself and put these appointments into your calendar. When you interview yourself, do it alone. Do it somewhere you find inspiring. This could be a beautiful coffee shop with a great vibe, the atrium of a gorgeous art gallery or in your home. Before you begin, switch your phone and computer off. This is your time, your space to focus exclusively on you. Make each of these dates a special occasion. Perhaps buy yourself a beautiful pen and journal for this project. Provide yourself with a small treat: maybe your favourite hot drink and a piece of sumptuous chocolate or a healthy snack bar at the start of each session. Light a candle. Burn your favourite incense. The idea is to create a space in your life that is sacred time dedicated entirely on you.

Know that you deserve this space. And when you take the time to fill up your own cup, you become much more peaceful and at ease in the world. The effects ripple out to all those around you. It is really quite magical. When you are on an aircraft, the instruction is always to put the oxygen mask on yourself first before helping anyone else. This is the very same idea.

Do not be tempted to merely *think* of the answers; write them down. Use pen and paper. This will draw you into the moment and help you to be clearer with your answers. If you are worried that someone will find what you write and read it, you could write on sheets of paper and then burn them afterwards.

A trick that I learned from an artist friend, Amanda Grace, is to write constantly without leaving gaps between your words. I challenge anyone to read that! Ideally, it would be good to keep your answers safe so that you could look back in a year's time and see how far you have progressed.

The very process of thinking about these questions and then writing the answers down is extraordinarily powerful.

Questionnaire

Before you begin:

- Take a few deep relaxing breaths or listen to the short audio-guided meditation available on www.healingcreations.ie.

- Of course some questions may not apply. Just answer the ones that do.

- Allow your answers to simply come. Let yourself be open as you can in your sacred and safe space.

- Why did you buy or pick up this book?

- Are you happy?

- If not, what do you believe you need to be happy?

- How many minutes or hours per day do you estimate you spend in worry or rumination?

- What do you love doing, even when you are tired or busy? Why?

- Are you unhappy in a relationship or job? Why?

- What do you like about this relationship or job? For example, does the paycheck make you feel safe? Or does the relationship save you from facing a fear of being alone?

- What do you fear about leaving this job or relationship?

- What do you believe is possible for you in life?

- Imagine you've just won the lottery. Now that money is no object, what will you do with your life?

- Bearing in mind how you answered the previous question, how can you start living your ideal life, even in the smallest of ways?

- What gifts, talents, or passions have you been hiding from yourself and the world?

- What can you do to start using your talents more often?

- What have you done in your life that you are most proud of?

- What kind of legacy do you want to leave behind?

- What would you like people to say about you at your funeral?

- How does your presence in the world help humanity?

- How would you like to help and serve humanity?

- To your best knowledge, how do other people perceive you?

- How would you like others to perceive you?

- If something you don't like happens, or things don't go as expected, how do you react?

- Do you hold grudges?

- How confident are you in your ability to make decisions for yourself?

- What is your biggest self-limiting belief?

- Who is the most important person in your life?

- Who is a person that you don't like, but yet you spend time with?

- What is true for you no matter what?

- What role does gratitude play in your life?

- What is your relationship with time?

- Do you believe your destiny is predetermined or that it is in your hands to shape and mould however you wish?

Well done! You have taken the time to get to know yourself. This is a brave, positive step in moving forward.

After completing this exercise, you will have gained a much better picture of where you are at and where it is that you want to go. Some key things will likely have jumped out at you. Perhaps you realise that fear or negative self-talk holds you back, or that a job or relationship needs to change.

Attempting to change everything at once is seductive but unrealistic. A more sustainable approach is to consistently make small changes. The remainder of this book is aimed at giving you the tools to move forward so that you can work on the aspects of yourself you want to improve. When we work on ourselves to bring light into our lives and heal what needs to be healed, external things in the world around us fall into place more easily.

Over time, the small changes that you make will compound and become significant changes. Like a snowball rolling and becoming bigger, you will slowly become stronger and more confident. You will begin moving towards your goals, enjoying each step along the way.

Many believe that their lives are predestined and that they should resign themselves to their lot in life. They may also think they cannot change a particular aspect of themselves. Yet the truth is that it is up to them to decide what that destiny will be and what they want to be in the world.

You must take responsibility. You are born with a unique life purpose, and it is up to you whether or not to say yes to taking action towards your most authentic self. In the same way you choose what to eat, who to keep company with and what to wear each day, choosing to say yes to your destiny is a decision that can only be realised when you take action to make that choice a reality.

No matter what you believe your destiny is – to be a mother, a businesswoman, an artist, a pioneer, a sportswoman – saying yes to your destiny is only the first step. While manifesting your dreams starts with knowing what you want and having faith that you can attain your goals, there are further steps that must be taken and decisions to be made before your destiny can truly happen.

Looking at the road ahead can be overwhelming. You may ask yourself, how on earth will I ever get there? But small steps each day add up. For example, if I think too much about writing this entire book, I feel anxiety and panic. But if I relax into the moment and reach my daily target of seven hundred words per day, then I enjoy the writing. And the next time I look at the word count, suddenly I'm at twenty thousand words. Each journey, each goal, begins with one step.

Being in the moment allows you to appreciate each stage of your progress, and when you look up one day, you'll suddenly realise how far you travelled without even knowing it. This can entail either moving towards a goal or improving an aspect of yourself. You are taking responsibility and you begin to act each day with the intention of doing so. Doorways begin to open for you, and each choice you make is a creative act toward realising your true self and living your goals and dreams. You become more in tune with your instincts and intuition. You recognise opportunities when they are presented to you and you are no longer afraid to seize those golden moments. You also begin to have awareness of the decisions or people that may not serve your greater vision and can more easily put them aside.

You are moving towards becoming your authentic self because you want to, not because you have to or someone else told you to. This makes a huge difference. When you are no longer under the thumb of obligation, obstacles that appear on your path become challenges to be embraced and overcome, and the journey with all its learning experiences becomes an adventure in which you are a willing partner. Your fate is in your hands. And your hands are very capable.

Summary

- What do you want to change? You may have a dream you want to fulfil, but aren't quite clear about it or where you want to go with it.
- The questionnaire in this chapter is a brilliant exercise to do once or twice a year. It will give you a starting point for living in alignment with who you truly are.
- When we work on ourselves to bring light into our lives and heal what needs to be healed, external things in the world around us fall into place more easily.
- You must take responsibility. You are born with a unique life purpose, and it is up to you whether or not to say yes to taking action towards your most authentic self.
- Being in the moment allows you to appreciate each stage of your progress, and when you look up one day, you'll suddenly realise how far you travelled without even knowing it.

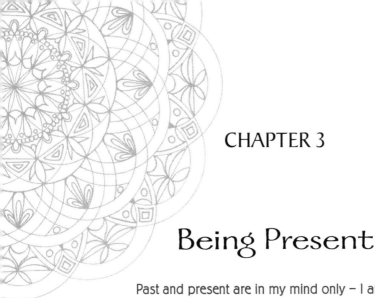

CHAPTER 3

Being Present

Past and present are in my mind only – I am now.

SRI NISARGADATTA MAHARAJ

The practice of mindful presence was the beginning of my journey of self-awareness and growth. It started with a decision to try and become present with my daughter during her bedtime story. It took a few weeks before I could integrate it fully, but finally my efforts paid off. I was amazed at how well it worked, and I could feel the magical power behind it. I could also sense the increased connection between my daughter and myself. I felt better. She felt better. It was then it dawned on me that if mindful presence could be that powerful in one situation, couldn't it be as powerful in others?

Being yourself

Simple acts of presence give you the space to be yourself. When I expanded my mindfulness to other areas, I seemed to have infinitely more time to do the things I loved rather than spending my time worrying and overthinking everything. I came to know myself better and to understand and appreciate the loving relationships and beautiful things that surrounded me. With this new awareness, I also began to perceive habits, relationships and other things that were not serving me. These I took note of and addressed at appropriate times.

Being peaceful

In a busy, ever-changing world, sometimes we just want things to stay the same. This is completely understandable – we can get overwhelmed with the amount of things that are thrown at us every day. Therefore, that desire for constancy must be satisfied from within ourselves. When you use the practice of mindful presence, it really moves you towards that sweet spot of stillness. Of course there will be times when things trigger you, but you will be aware of these triggers because you will have at your disposal a toolkit to get you back into alignment more quickly. Presence is a wonderful thing to bring into your life and it will help you so much with what you want to achieve, be that an external goal or an internal goal – plus you will be in general more happy and experience less worry.

Being more productive

The idea of women as multitaskers par excellence is perpetuated in the media. We are often proud of being able to do so many things at the one time, but this does not necessarily mean we are more productive.

Also, we are most definitely not present when we are multitasking.

Multitasking can cause us to feel overwhelmed and distracted. When we do it, the levels of the stress hormone cortisol increases in our bodies. Stress can ensue from our tasks not being properly finished or done well. The next time you catch yourself on a womanly multitasking binge, check in with how you are feeling. Notice the sensations in your body. How is your breathing? Is your heart rate fast? Is there a knot in your stomach or tension in your shoulders? Are your muscles tight?

It is better to break down your jobs into manageable chunks. If you can spend three-quarters of an hour or half an hour working on each task with complete focus, then you will have a better chance of being more productive overall.

You can practise being present with any activity you choose. For example, when I am creating art, I turn or switch off every communication device, light a candle and incense and immerse myself in my work without distraction. When I do that, I find my creativity is much better and I am more at ease. If I am trying to create and work at other things at the same time, everything suffers. Now obviously we cannot do that with every activity and that's OK. As a mother, I know that only too well. But finding simple things throughout your day to be present with is powerful.

Build up your presence muscle gradually, one task or situation at a time. Setting an intention to focus on the particular job or event at hand is a great way to start. Pick something that is going to happen today and set an intention to be present while engaged in that particular activity or task. It can be anything: a trip to the cinema or park, a meal with friends, a conversation with your friend, partner or child, washing the dishes . . .

When we become present with activities, people and tasks in our lives, we naturally become much more aware of how we are actually feeling during those acts. This can be very enlightening. It is another way to really get to know your strengths, your fears, your insecurities, what makes you happy and what doesn't. When you are present try to bear witness without judgement as to how you are feeling in a particular moment. Observe with curiosity how you are being and feeling in different situations.

Being discerning

Sometimes in a situation you may find yourself feeling angry or jealous or some other emotion that either society or you deem as being wrong. These are actually natural feelings, so try not to make a wrongness of them. Rather say, for example: 'That's interesting, this situation or person is making me experience anger. I can feel it in my chest area and my shoulders feel tense. I am going to allow myself to be curious about why that is happening to me.'

Try not to blame other people for your emotions. If you do, you give away your power to change and to heal. Becoming aware of the feelings that are happening within in real time shines a light upon them and allows you to look more closely at why you are experiencing them.

A question you can ask yourself is: 'Is it useful for me to have this emotion in this situation?' For example, anger is most probably a waste of energy if you are in a traffic jam. But perhaps in a different situation it can be useful. If you were about to be physically assaulted, anger would provide the force needed to help protect yourself.

Think about the times when you considered an emotion you were experiencing as a bad feeling when it might in fact have been good and useful. If the emotion is not suited to the situation you are currently in, you could say to yourself: 'Anger can be useful to me in some situations, but this is not one of them. Right now it is simply draining my energy.' Then take three deep breaths in through the nose and out through the mouth and become present and aware of other things around you.

In your own time take out your journal and write with abandon about these feelings. Really delve in and maybe refer back to some of the questions in Chapter 2 which may help you discover more about yourself.

Here are several simple exercises that you can try each day to bring the art of being present into your life. Remember, it will not happen immediately, but like everything you have to learn, it takes a little practice, so go easy on yourself. As your practices become integrated into your life, you will become happier and more appreciative of what you have. Lastly, don't forget to listen to your inner guidance system (p. 23) regarding what feels good and right for you.

Exercises

1) Being present while showering

Showering mindfully is personally one of my favourite things and makes for a very positive start to the day.

When you have a shower, feel the water against your body. Notice how it feels as it touches your skin gently or strongly, and how hot or cold it is. Pay attention to the sound the water makes when it hits the curtains or tiles. Feel the soap bar or sponge against your skin and smell your showering products. Notice how it feels when you wash your hair and your body. Feel the lather in your fingers. Imagine you are washing away any worries or tension from your body and see them flow away down the plughole. Lastly, visualise the water as bright cleansing warm light flowing down through and around you. Not a bad way to start the day!

2) Being present while eating

This is one I am still working on! Often I cannot remember what I ate for my last meal. Can you remember?

For one meal per day or even per week, concentrate on mindfully eating your food. No television, no phone, no book, no newspaper. Chew your food slowly. Take small bites. Smell the food. Admire the colours and textures. Let the food linger in your mouth to savour the flavours. Think of how this food came to be at your table. Think of the growers of the food and those who harvested it, produced it, packaged it, transported it, and stocked it in the shop where you bought it. If you did not buy the food, think of the person who did. Then think of all of the utensils and power and invention that it took to cook your food, and the effort that was taken to present it. This is a beautiful way to see the inter-relatedness of humanity and how a system works so harmoniously. You will begin to feel a sense of gratitude rippling through you.

3) Being present while commuting

Have you ever driven somewhere and had no recollection of what route you took?

Choose to do this exercise for your morning or evening commute. Become aware of your surroundings in the bus, train or car. Notice the textures of the seats. Look at the trees, the sky, the houses and buildings nearby. Bring your awareness to the other vehicles and people around you. If you drive, pay attention to the pressure your foot uses against the pedal to accelerate or stop. Feel the steering wheel between your hands and the texture of it. Listen to the sounds around you.

Become aware of how you feel when there is traffic. Are you stressed, anxious or angry? If so, how is your body reacting? Where in your body do you feel it? If you can, remove yourself from your thoughts and emotions and bring your attention to your breath. Traffic is not desirable, but being stuck in it doesn't have to automatically put you in a bad mood. It is a situation that you cannot control. Anger and stress merely depletes your energy. If you find yourself regularly stuck in traffic, ask: 'How might I use this time more beneficially?' Most cars these days have good audio systems that you could use to learn a language or listen to a book you have been meaning to read. Begin to use the time as a benefit rather than a chore. Let the commute be a time for personal growth.

4) Being present in conversation

Think of the last time you had a great conversation with somebody. While most probably an interesting topic contributed to this, it is also very likely that the person you had this conversation with was a good and mindful listener. Decide on a moment of the day and a person with whom you will practise this exercise.

Pay attention to the person talking to you. Maintain eye contact with them as much as possible. Be attentive to their body language. Resist the urge to interrupt or think of what you are going to reply to them while they are talking. Give them your full attention. This means putting away the phone and stopping whatever else you may be doing. If there are other things getting in the way, postpone the exercise until you can find a more suitable situation.

When practicing mindful conversations, become aware of how you feel during and after speaking to people. Some people will leave you feeling motivated and energised. With others it will be neutral,

WHO WOULD YOU BE IF . . .

and with yet others you will feel drained of energy, or perhaps you did not feel comfortable sharing your successes or worries with them. It is very empowering to be aware of how different people make you feel. Make a conscious choice to spend more time with people who energise and uplift you, whilst cutting down on your time spent with those who leave you drained or limited.

5) Being present while waiting

Throughout your day you will often find yourself waiting for something or somebody. This is a great opportunity to practice mindful presence. Examples are: queuing at a bus stop or in a department store, waiting for a delayed train or plane, sitting waiting for ages in a doctor's full waiting room, or waiting to meet that friend who is always late.

Notice how you feel when you see a long queue in the store ahead of you. How does your body react? Do you tense up? Are you angry or annoyed? Notice where you feel tension in your body. Ask yourself: 'Is the way I feel at the moment useful to me or anybody else?' If you can, pull your attention away from your thoughts and emotions. Be aware of your breath. Breathe three times deeply in through your nose and out through your mouth. Now really begin to notice what is around you. Become aware of the sounds, the colours and the textures. Practise compassion for the person or thing that is making you wait and remember it will sometimes be you who will be making others wait.

6) Being Present while cleaning

Cleaning has become an activity I now actually enjoy. I used to get annoyed at having to do it but now I use it as a time to practise mindfulness and also to cherish and give gratitude for my home.

Let's take folding the laundry as one example. Observe everything you possibly can as you move through the motions of the task at hand. Notice the texture of the fabrics. Really see the patterns on various items of clothing. Feel the softness of the fabrics when they are fresh out of the dryer or from the clothes line. Bring awareness to the colours of the clothing, and maybe create new ways of stacking or arranging your clothes together. If the clothes are fresh out of a dryer, feel the heat coming from the clothes. Feel any static moving through the air. Observe how different materials feel, and notice each and every detail as you fold shirt after shirt and sock after sock. Take a deep breath after you have finished folding the clothes, offering gratitude that you have clean clothes to fold and wear, and beautiful clean fresh sheets to sleep on.

Other examples could be when you are cleaning your kitchen, bathroom or vacuuming the floors. With these different chores you could visualise scrubbing, sweeping or hoovering away any negative energy and replacing it with clean clear vitalised energy.

7) Being present in nature

Throughout the entire day, take time to notice the natural world around you.

See the colours of the leaves, the shapes of the trees. Notice the beautiful cloud formations and hues in the sky. Look at the birds, the moon and the stars. You can do this even if you are in a city. Take a little time each day to go for a walk or run in a forest, park or on a beach. Surrounding yourself by nature is a great way to replenish your body, re-awaken creative energy, clear your mind and unplug from the many technological distractions that we have in today's world.

We often use the term, 'go out into nature'. That sounds as though we are somehow separate from nature, that we ourselves are not 'natural' – especially those of us living in cities. By taking deliberate time out in the urban, suburban or rural environment, we reclaim our relationship with the natural world around us.

8) Mindfulness meditation

One of the best ways to enhance your ability to focus is mindfulness meditation. The practice of focusing your attention on something like your breath, refocusing each time your mind wanders, is an excellent way to strengthen your attention muscle. Meditation teaches you to become aware of when you are distracted, so you can bring your attention back to the task at hand. You learn to notice your thoughts and emotions without getting carried away by them.

An audio meditation that accompanies this chapter is available on www.healingcreations.ie

You will find as you practise mindful presence that your awareness of what you enjoy as well as what you do not enjoy will be highlighted. Get creative and think up your own ways to practise. Maya Angelou famously said, 'If you don't like something, change it. If you can't change it, change your attitude.'

Your mindful practice is indeed about changing your attitude. But perhaps there is also an opportunity for physical changes in the situations that you find yourself. For example, I used to shop at a supermarket where the hard-to-negotiate car park would leave me in a lather of sweat and muttering curses. I would come home feeling tense. When I began the practice of mindful presence I became much more aware of how bad this place was making me feel. Could I change that? Yes, I could change my attitude to it. But there was also another option: I could find a supermarket with a car park that was easier to get around. And that was what I did!

> If you don't like something, change it. If you can't change it, change your attitude.
>
> Maya Angelou

Often in life we operate on autopilot. We do something because that is the way we have always done it or because that is the way others around us do that particular thing. Your practice of mindful presence will highlight these areas in your life. Take a look at your day and see if you can find some small things that you really do not enjoy doing or working at. Write them down in your notebook. Now, is there a way to do them differently? Or not do them at all?

Mindful presence can be brought into any aspect of your life. Doing it in a way that feels good to you is important, as then you have much more of a chance of making it habitual. Have fun. Make it your own.

Summary

- Simple acts of presence give you the space to be yourself.

- Build up your presence muscle gradually, one task or situation at a time.

- Try not to blame other people for your emotions. If you do, you give away your power to change and to heal.

- You will find as you practise mindful presence that your awareness of what you enjoy as well as what you do not enjoy will be highlighted.

- As your practices of the exercises in this chapter become integrated into your life, you will become happier and more appreciative of what you have.

CHAPTER 4

Time Out

I have realised that the past and future are real illusions,
that they exist in the present, which is what there is
and all there is.
ALAN WATTS

What, you might ask, has time got to do with anything here? The thing is, many of us worry about time a lot. Excessively, even. So often I hear women complaining of not having enough time in their days, uttering familiar phrases like, 'Time flies', 'If only I had the time', 'The clock is ticking'. Do you find yourself saying, 'I'll never have enough time to get this or that done?' or, 'I'd write that book or paint that painting, if only I had the time.' When I teach art workshops, I often see people getting anxious about time. Will they have enough time to finish their piece? They speed ahead at a breakneck pace in case they don't!

Focusing on time or lack thereof creates an enormous distraction in our minds. Have you noticed that when you anxiously await a phone call or text it tends not to arrive? Then you give up and like magic the call comes or the text appears. Have you also noticed that hurrying frustrates you, leads to mistakes, and can actually slow you down? Are you aware that worrying about what might happen, instead of taking appropriate actions or preventive measures, only serves to waste your energy?

These are a few examples typifying our strained relationship with time. Many of us are constantly thinking about what happened yesterday and anticipating what is going to happen tomorrow. They are not being present in their lives. Constantly doing this cuts us off from the beauty of life, which only ever manifests in the present moment.

Time in our minds

Time is both our limitation and our opportunity. Can you remember what happened yesterday? Think of one particular thing. As it turns out, it did not really happen yesterday. It happened in yesterday's *present moment*. That is the exact moment that is happening right now. The present moment is the only place where anything can ever happen. Ever! And that concept is worth paying attention to because your happiness is directly correlated with your awareness of it.

Think of a particular thing that happened to you one hour ago. Now look around you. Is it still happening? The chances are, it isn't, or at least not the exact same version of it. What happened an hour ago is utterly unique and will never occur again – just like what is happening right now will never happen again.

Both the past and future only exist in your mind as thought patterns.

In fact, literally anything that is not in this moment only exists in your mind: your to-do list, bills that need paying, something that someone said to you and that you are mulling over. None of it is truly real. That doesn't mean you should lock yourself into the lotus position, stay still and be completely in this moment, never moving again! Our minds need to think ahead to get things done. We enjoy planning for our futures and reliving pleasurable memories. Indeed it is powerful to visualise your future and how you want it to be, and you will be doing a lot of that later on in the book. Of course you also need to pay your bills, or your future 'now' won't appreciate it very much!

> Both the past and future only exist in your mind as thought patterns.

How we experience time shifts and morphs according to how we are experiencing that moment. Time is a concept and a very useful one at that. It allows us measure reality based on the revolution and rotation of the planets around the sun. This is useful to us for recording history, growing crops and making it to work, appointments or school on time. But obsession with time comes at a cost. One of the most basic facts about time is that, even though we insist on measuring it as though it were an objective unit, it doesn't, in many conditions, feel as if it is moving at the same pace. Five minutes can feel like an hour; ten hours can feel like five minutes. A decade can pass like two years. Two years can seem like half a century.

The two meanings of time

The ancient Greeks had two words for time. The first was *chronos*, which we still use today in words like chronological, chronic, and synchronised. It refers to linear clock time – the time that is measured by the planet's rotation. The second was *kairos*. *Kairos* is qualitative: it measures moments, not seconds. It is to do with the idea of the perfect moment, the opportune moment to take action on something. Interestingly, the ancient Indians in Asia also divided time into two distinct categories with similar notions named *kala* and *ritu*.

Many of us have a tendency to become time-driven; our lives can revolve entirely around time. We live almost exclusively by *chronos* time in Western culture. Perhaps it is because we don't have a word for *kairos* in our language and so the concept is not imbued into our consciousness. We are always looking for the next thing to do or putting our dreams off until some distant time in the future. 'When I get that house, I'll be happy.' 'I can't wait to finish this, so I can relax.' 'I'll write that book when I retire.'

Become aware of the relationship you have with time. Begin to bring the concept of time into your journaling practice. If you catch yourself making time-related statements, jot them down. Don't judge yourself harshly – wc all do it!

Learning to work with time

The work from the previous chapter on being mindful and being in the present moment will gradually help you to have more moments of *kairos.* In these moments the quality of time changes. You will begin to notice a shift in your relationship with your inner guidance system (see p. 23), which will help you to move towards your authentic self, goals and dreams. You will learn to know the right time to act on something, or to say something.

You will begin to find yourself in the right place at the right time or speaking to the right person at the exact opportune moment. You will experience more coincidences or synchronicities that can show you that you are on the right path. For me, synchronicity is like *chronos* and *kairos* kissing . . . the two forms of time coming together in a perfect moment.

To enter this state of flow between *chronos* and *kairos*, it is helpful to dig deeply to understand and clear out what is at the root of any anxiety you may hold around time. Do you over-schedule yourself? If so, why? Why do you want to be so busy? And why does it seem so normal in our society to worry about time so much? Our societal norm is to do our very best to lengthen our lives by striving to add more years to it, usually by eating more greens and wheatgerm, going to bed early, and jumping up and down in the gym. There is a multibillion euro industry based entirely on our fear of ageing and death. Many of these things are good for us, others not so much, but old age and death cannot reliably be warded off with green smoothies and face cream. The inevitable will come. The best way to lengthen your life is not by attempting to stick more years on to the end of it, but rather to become more fully present in the moments that we do have, appreciating them fully.

When you ask most people how they are, the response will generally be, 'Oh busy, busy!' It would be almost weird if someone responded, 'Oh I'm great, I've all the time in the world.' Notice how often you talk about time when you have conversations with friends or family. The way that Western society is organised means we are constantly caught up in a drama about time. It works well for a capitalist model of society. It keeps us busy buying, working, spending and doing. What happens on the macro level of our society will be mirrored on the micro level, that is, within ourselves. So what might the payoff be for worrying about time on a personal level?

> Notice how often you talk about time when you have conversations with friends or family.

Blaming time

When I examined this question for myself, I saw that the more I complained about time, the more it gave me an excuse not to do a thing that could scare me. Most likely that would be something that would push me out of my comfort zone. When I was initially asked to write this book, my immediate response was, 'Oh, I'd never have the time. I'm a mother, an artist, a teacher. I have so many balls in the air already. How could I possibly do this?' The excuse and illusion of not having enough time could have proved a great mechanism to keep me 'safe'. 'Safe' from trying something new and challenging. It required a concerted inner mental push to change my way of thinking and ultimately I found I did in fact have enough time.

We all have a lot of dreams that we have accomplished, but there are also many ideas that fall by the wayside in the name of 'not having enough time'. Putting ourselves out there more fully means we have to face things we want to avoid. A big one is the potential for rejection. And rejection is one of our deepest fears. Similarly, a friend of mine bravely admitted that for her, complaining about time was related to ego. The 'I'm too busy' story can indeed stoke the ego: 'Oh, look at me – busy, busy, busy!'

A recent workshop participant shared her new awareness that lack of time gave her an excuse and an outside source for not following her dreams. She said, 'I never thought that I was the one to blame. I don't blame people, not very often anyway . . . but today I suddenly realised that I've actually been blaming time. My current belief is that I don't have enough time, and that's why I haven't tried new things or followed particular dreams. When I blame time, it implies that it's not my fault. Wow. This has been a big discovery for me!'

Time and self-reflection

Your constant busyness could also be stopping you from having to deal with grief, trauma or a bad relationship. So allow yourself the time to look within. Give yourself more moments of *kairos*. It is a place where you can honour these wounds, apply a salve and begin to heal. If you have an issue that needs to be dealt with and you are finding it difficult to face, reach out. Find a professional you can relate to. You can move through this with grace and the right help.

Becoming aware of your relationship with time is powerful. When you are journaling, look at where you waste time doing things that you don't actually enjoy. Are you being busy for the sake of being busy? Are you doing things simply because others around you are doing the same thing? I often hear mothers complaining that all their time is swallowed up in bringing their children to this place and that place, as well as to multiple after-school activities. Other women become involved in so many groups and activities that they don't have a moment for themselves. If you identify with this, think about it. Do you or your children really need to do all of those things, or are you doing them simply because it has become the norm? Or maybe you are in the habit of whiling away time watching TV, gaming or constantly browsing social media. Would it be so terrible to stop doing so many things – or might it actually help?

Busyness is one thing, but we can be bored too. This ostensibly means that we can't find anything to do that interests us. But where are we looking? Again, outside ourselves. The essence of boredom is that we actually have nothing with which to distract ourselves from ourselves. We are stuck with nothing but our own mind, body and spirit to pay attention to. Constant busyness and doing conditions us to not to experience ourselves or our own company. And why would we? We probably view ourselves as not particularly interesting.

The truth is, when you allow space and time for yourself it gives you a chance for self-reflection and creativity. It enables you to become authentic and happier doing things that you love. Giving children free time gifts them the chance to play, develop and evolve, and very importantly, to become themselves. The same applies to us grown women. When we are busy all the time, our imaginations and creative capacities atrophy and die.

Since getting rid of my TV several years ago, I find I have infinitely more time and so much more creativity and inspiration. In the past I was prone to coming home from work, flicking on the TV and sitting in front of it for the entire evening. After all, I was tired after a long day at work. I deserved to relax, didn't I? But in reality I was stealing my own life away. Yes, of course, relaxation is important. But I was wasting whole tranches of time, perhaps five hours per night, which worked out at a whopping thirty-five hours per week. Wow! I had become particularly addicted to Big Brother at one juncture and one evening I remember turning it on to see that nobody in the Big Brother house was awake. The cameras were poised on a room full of snoozing duvets and there I was on my sofa waiting for one of them to move and get up. I had a Eureka moment then, a moment of clarity, where I realised that what I was doing was very unhealthy.

> When we are busy all the time, our imaginations and creative capacities atrophy and die.

If you can learn to stop blaming time for not getting things done or moving forward in life, that is a great step forward. However, if you still feel stuck, what could it be that is still holding you back?

For almost all of us, it is fear.

Summary

- Focusing on time or lack thereof creates an enormous distraction in our minds.

- The present moment is the only place where anything can ever happen, and that concept is worth paying attention to because your happiness is directly correlated with your awareness of it.

- The ancient Greeks had two words for time. The first was *chronos*, which refers to the time that is measured by the planet's rotation. The second was *kairos*, which measures moments, not seconds. It is to do with the idea of the perfect moment, the opportune moment to take action on something.

- The best way to lengthen your life is not by attempting to stick more years on to the end of it, but rather to become more fully present in the moments that we do have, appreciating them fully.

- The way that Western society is organised means we are constantly caught up in a drama about time. It keeps us busy buying, working, spending and doing.

- The excuse and illusion of not having enough time can prove a great mechanism to keep you 'safe'. 'Safe' from trying something new and challenging.

- When you allow space and time for yourself it gives you a chance for self-reflection and creativity.

CHAPTER 5

Making Friends
with Fear

I'm not afraid of storms, for I'm learning how to sail my ship.
LOUISA MAY ALCOTT

We can be afraid of so many things. However, having a healthy relationship with fear is important in the journey to living a peaceful and fulfilled life.

Fear can be constricting, holding us back from doing the things that we really want to do. We can be afraid of what other people think of us, whether we are we good enough, or of doing something wrong. We can have a fear of judgement, a fear of not attaining our goals, a fear of ridicule, a fear of failure – on and on it goes.

If we harbor and feed these fears within us, it is hard to move forward in our lives, make changes and grow to be the best person we can be. Fear closes us down and prevents us from even *trying* to work on ourselves.

It is actually perfectly natural for us to default into these fear habits.

Our brains are hardwired to find the negative – that is what keeps us safe. The capacity to emphasise the negative over the positive is an evolutionary phenomenon. From our earliest beginnings, being aware of and avoiding danger has been a critical survival skill. This trait has served us well. It is what triggers our fight or flight response, keeping us safe. The amygdala, also known as the 'old brain', kicks into action when we perceive danger. It releases cortisol through our bodies. Our heart rate speeds up. Our palms may begin to sweat and our hands begin to shake.

There are two basic types of fear:

1) **Healthy fear** – This is a response to physical danger and helps to keep us safe and protected.
   Example: You are standing on a roof that is very slippery. You are afraid. You climb down carefully.

2) **Unhealthy fear** – This is where we are constantly running through various scenarios of what could go wrong in particular situations.
   Example: You would like to write a blog on your travel experiences. It is going to be epic! It is a brilliant idea and you are so excited. For two whole minutes. Then you begin to go through all sorts of reasons why it could go wrong. What would your work colleagues think? Who are you to be writing a blog on travel anyway? What if nobody reads it? What if it is total rubbish?

Our brains react to fear in these ways naturally. Remember, it wants to keep you safe and so it defaults to this ancient mechanism.

Talk to your fear

Conjure up the feeling you had when thinking of a great idea you had about something. You were delighted and enthusiastic. Then fear crept in. But now that you are aware of what is happening, allow the fear in, allow it to engage with you. Ask yourself: Is this a healthy or an unhealthy fear? Become well acquainted with fear. Know it. Talk to it. Question it.

A fun mindful way is to talk to your fear as if it is a real person. I call my fear Boris. I imagine him as a large, rather overbearing person wearing an unkempt suit. He always seems to have his arms folded. He does a lot of eye rolling. He smokes a great deal and is very opinionated.

What does your Boris look like? See him or her standing there. Really visualise the character. If you like, draw a picture of him or her. Get to know your Boris intimately. Talk to your Boris!

This is a conversation Boris and I are having right now:

Me: I'm writing a book on mindfulness and personal development. I have loads of ideas and experiences I want to write about. I've lived through many things and learned so much as I've progressed. I have also grown and changed in ways I could never have imagined. I see so many people struggling and I would love to share with them what I have learned along the road so far. This could be really cool. This book could really help people. I've been given a gift here, something that would be of value to others. Yes! I'm going to do it! I've always wanted to do something like this since my journey began.

Boris: Hah! You a writer. Are you joking? Remember that time in college when the tutor told you your essay was a pile of crap? What was the mark you got again? A 'D', was it? Almost failed there, didn't you?

Me: Thank you for reminding me of that, Boris. I know you are trying to keep me safe. But that was only one time. Remember the prize that I won for creative writing? And that time I had a piece published in the paper and all the lovely mails I received after that? Remember that, Boris? And what about the blog? People seem to love the blog.

Boris: Oh, but you get plenty of 'unsubscribes', don't you? It's not that great, you know. A book, huh! What would the people at work think about your grand plans? That day when you talked about this stuff they changed the subject and began talking about some reality TV show. Some of them would just love to see you fail. If this is a pile of crap they will be delighted! Are you going to give them the opportunity to laugh at you and ridicule you? Just imagine the conversations they would have. Do you really think anybody is going to be interested in what you have to say? Come on. Get real. People want to hear from real experts. And. You. Are. Not. One.

Me: Yes, I recall that time at work, Boris. What does their opinion matter to me anyway? That's their own stuff. That day at break time, people were just tired and cranky after the morning meeting. No one really wanted to be getting all serious at coffee. Anyway, Vivienne came up to me later on and asked me for advice on dealing with a situation she was having with her husband. And then a couple of weeks later she thanked me because she said I really helped her.

Boris: Oh yeah. Do you really think Vivienne took on board anything you said?

Me: Actually, Vivienne is very self-aware. She is someone who wants to make a change in her life and not just complain and do nothing. You know, Boris, there are plenty of people who need this book. They want to hear from someone like them, a real person who has had many fears and challenging experiences. They want to read about how someone worked through stuff, understood their fears and learned from them. For sure you could learn from people who have sat through lectures and courses and got a bit of paper at the end of them. That's all great. But you need to live it too. Anyway, I have some bits of paper, fat lot of good they are though.

I know you mean well. You are a great friend, and I really appreciate you trying to protect me. But you know what? I am going to give this a try! Here's a great quote from Samuel Beckett: 'Ever tried. Ever failed. No matter. Try again. Fail again. Fail better.'

Boris: Right so, don't say I didn't warn you.

Boris has a negative opinion on just about everything. Here he is piping in again!

Boris: You shouldn't be writing this book if you have a Boris.

Me: So are there people out there with no fear inside them? No Boris or Borisette inside them at all? That would be a bit scary actually. Remember the time the building scaffolding nearly fell on little Rebecca and you nudged me and I grabbed her out of the way? She could have been really seriously injured, or worse. God, Boris, I love you sometimes! I really do.

Do you also recall the time when we first met properly? I didn't know your name then. I was getting divorced and you were telling me there was no way I could do all the paperwork, that I wouldn't be able. That it would be much safer to stay where I was. That I could end up homeless and alone. You said I wouldn't be able to parent my daughter properly if I was on my own. We really got to know each other then, didn't we, Boris?

And look, I did it all and it worked out so well! I know now you were very kind to be thinking of me and trying to protect me. I enjoy our chats now, I have to say. We can really work together on things so I can move forward and make the life I want for myself.

Make friends with your fear. Have a healthy relationship with it. Keep the communication channels open between you both, just like in any healthy relationship. My Boris is with me all the way, even in writing this book. By chatting with him, and the two of us getting well acquainted, I now know the difference between healthy fear that keeps me safe and unhealthy fear that keeps me from moving forward.

Boris sometimes comes to tell me many so-called 'home truths' about myself. But when we chat, I realise that many of these 'home truths' are not at all true. They are simply fears and insecurities I have picked up along the way. By realising this, remembering back to the times when I have felt this way before, I have started to move forward with my life in the direction that I have always wanted. I have been able to change my marriage situation, my home, my career from a librarian to an artist – which had been my dream since I was a child – and now I am a writer as well!

You can do this too. You absolutely can make the changes in your life to make it the life that you want to live. You can live a true and authentic life where you can look back from your deathbed and say, 'I am so happy I did all or most of the things that I have always wanted to do.'

I will hold hands with Boris to the very end, because I have no doubt he will be whispering in my ear then too. But we will be friends.

Exercises

1) Create your own fear character.

Give your fear a name. Really imagine and visualise his or her height, facial features, hair, age and clothes. Give him or her a trait that makes you laugh: a mad hat or maybe a colourful dotty dicky bow. Make them things that ensure you won't take him or her too seriously!

2) Develop a safe friendship with your Boris.

Alongside conversations with your Boris, you need to be compassionate with yourself. You need to give yourself a feeling of safety, nurturing, love and acceptance. Tell yourself that it is OK to be afraid. It is OK that Boris is in the room. However, he is not someone to be scared of anymore. I mean, look at his hat! You hadn't spoken for years, if ever, with Boris, but now you are becoming friends. So it's all OK.

3) Understand your fear as insecurity.

Another way to look at fear is to see it as insecurity. You are insecure when you have fearful thoughts. What would you do if you had a scared child in front of you? You would try to make him or her feel safe any way you could, right? You would comfort the child. You would tell them everything is OK. So now bring it back to you. Care for your insecurity in the same way, both in your mind and in physical terms. Talk to it using your own name or a pet name that you had as a child.

4) After working through a fear, treat yourself.

After you have a successful heart-to-heart talk with your Boris about a particular fear, you deserve to celebrate. Go take a warm bubble bath. Or go for a run. Watch an old movie. Go and get a back massage. Do something you love, and really learn to look after yourself.

Summary

- Fear can be constricting, holding us back from doing the things that we really want to do.
- There are two basic types of fear:

  1) Healthy fear – This is a response to physical danger and helps to keep us safe and protected.

  2) Unhealthy fear – This is where we are constantly running through various scenarios of what could go wrong in particular situations.
- A fun mindful way is to talk to your fear as if it is a real person.
- By making friends with your fear, you can live a true and authentic life where you can look back from your deathbed and say, 'I am so happy I did all or most of the things that I have always wanted to do.'

CHAPTER 6

Cultivating Resilience

Between stimulus and response there is a space.
In that space is our power to choose our response.
In our response lies our growth and our freedom.

VIKTOR FRANKL

Have you ever received a cutting comment from a person that left you feeling hurt and cut to the quick? A comment that stopped you from doing something you really wanted to do, or from saying something that you really wanted to say?

Many years ago I sang at the after-party of a wedding. I love to sing and am actually not all that bad. As I was singing I noticed a male acquaintance sniggering and muttering something under his breath to a friend who was sitting beside him. I took it personally, assuming he was commenting about my singing voice. I held onto that hurt tightly, and didn't sing in public after that.

Thankfully, I have learned a lot in the intervening years, and have recently begun working on this issue. I am really enjoying the process of healing and am looking forward to singing in public again in the near future. I do regret that I allowed it to stop me from doing something that I loved. For all I really knew, that man could have been sniggering and whispering about something entirely different! Had I understood resilience and how to flex that muscle then, there would have been a very different outcome.

Another place where resilience is extraordinarily useful is when you suffer a disappointing setback that keeps you from moving forward, for example, not getting that interview or being turned down for something you had really wanted to do.

> Resilience is about recognising when and how you are affected by pressure and having at hand a toolbox of coping strategies.

Resilience is the ability to bounce back from setbacks, adversity or negative situations with more ease and readiness, and is a remarkably powerful quality to embody in life. It allows you to face unforeseen events, obstacles and failures without allowing them to dominate, derail or ruin your life.

Resilience is not about being unaffected by stress or pressure; it is about recognising when and how you are affected by it and having at hand a toolbox of coping strategies. As you learn about and practise resilience, it can be continually increased and improved.

These days I can bounce back from difficult situations or negative comments more easily. That doesn't mean that I don't feel the intensity of the situation or problem any less keenly, but now I can deal with adversity more quickly and effectively. And if I can learn how to increase my resilience superpowers, so can you. No matter how old you are or what your situation is, all you need to do in order to increase your resilience is to have a willingness to do so.

It is worth noting at this point that as you begin to make positive changes in your life, you might find that people around you can appear unsupportive or negative. They might tell you all of the reasons you can't move ahead or even put obstacles in your way. People mean well. Their comments are not meant in any harmful way.

Remember, our brains want us to stay safe, to stay in the comfort zone – and that very thing is happening in your friends' brains too. Their Boris is speaking. If people whom you expected to be supportive of your journey are not, try not to share so much of your goals and dreams with them for now. Engage instead with those who uplift and support you. The others will come around in time.

The development of resilience will not happen overnight. It requires effort, commitment, awareness and focus. From doing the work in the previous chapters you will now be more aware of your inner thoughts and emotions in varying situations.

Exercise

Dealing with Negative Comments or Situations

* Resilience requires taking a moment after a particular negative stimulus hits you. Instead of immediately reacting, give

yourself a little space. Breathe. If you are agitated, perhaps do a short meditation.

- Then notice how you feel. Where in your body do you feel the hurt? Have you ever felt this way before? What was the first time you felt like this? Simply observe.

- Instead of blaming whomever or whatever, take full responsibility for how you are feeling right now. Allow it to be. Many of our emotional reactions to situations stem from something that happened in childhood and the memory has been stored in the clever computer bank that is your subconscious mind.

I recently received a comment on a social media post where I had shared one of my artworks. I had put a lot of effort and many hours into the painting. The comment was: 'It looks like a bitumen pizza, what are you sharing this rubbish for?'

I took time to notice how I felt. Not good! I could feel anxiety swirling in my belly. When had I felt like this before? I suddenly remembered back to when I was six years old. I was in school and trying to show a picture I had spent ages drawing to a teacher. She turned to me and said, 'What, what? I'm busy, go away, I've no time for this nonsense!' So that was it – I found the source of those feelings of rejection, fear and hurt regarding my art. And I knew now that if similar comments came in the future I would be better able to deal with them, and they would lose some of their power.

There was another thing to take into account: was the comment about my artwork on the social media post in any way constructive? No. Constructive criticism is a great thing and useful to take on board when it is offered to us. A good question to ask yourself when you get a negative or cutting comment is: has anything in my reality actually changed? In my case, the painting was still the same painting I had done and had thoroughly enjoyed creating.

Now either the image really did look like a bitumen pizza and I needed to improve, or it didn't. The comment was only powerful if somewhere deep inside I believed it to be true. Did I believe that the painting was rubbish? No I didn't. I loved the piece. Were the other comments about the piece negative? No, on the contrary, the twenty other comments on the social media post were positive and also contained great feedback.

> At the same time a resilient person is feeling, 'I'm upset about this', they are also thinking, 'but I'm grateful about that'.

A resilient person isn't denying the negative emotions of a situation. She is also not burying her head in the sand regarding the problem. Instead, they are letting these negative feelings sit side by side with other thoughts and feelings. At the same time they are feeling, 'I'm upset about this', they are also thinking, 'but I'm grateful about that'.

You may think, 'This sort of positive emotional response doesn't come naturally to me.' It didn't to me either. You can change that. It will, however, mean challenging your reflexive thoughts and your self-talk. Most of us automatically label circumstances and events in our everyday life as either good or bad. Now when you look at a particular situation that you are finding difficult, become aware if you are being harsh or overly self-critical. Are you expanding your mental torch onto the situation to see the bigger picture at hand and the positive aspects of it? Because there will always be a positive aspect, or something you can learn, if you look carefully enough.

Good thing, bad thing . . . who knows?

When you don't label something a good or bad thing, you don't suffer. This is a concept based in Buddhist philosophy and is used by psychologists to help people heal and accept challenges in their lives. Rather than encouraging us to decide whether something is good or bad, radical acceptance encourages us to simply accept things as they are.

The mystics say everything happens for a reason and that nothing is either good or bad but it is only our thinking that makes it so. The ancient Sufi story below illustrates the wisdom of reserving judgement, and of remaining in the present moment. It will help you avoid unnecessary stress and worry, and will give you the courage to move forward regardless. Here is the tale:

> Once upon a time there was an old farmer who lived in a valley with his son, a handsome and dutiful young man. They lived a

peaceful life and despite being poor, they were very happy. So much so that neighbours began to get envious and wanted to understand the secret of their happiness. They seemed always to be smiling, these two.

One day, the old man used all his meagre savings to buy a beautiful black stallion to help with work on the farm. The very same day he bought it, the horse jumped the fence and galloped off and away into the hills.

The neighbours came to express their concern. 'Oh, that's such an awful thing to happen! However are you going to plough the fields now? Isn't it such a dreadful thing to have happened?'

The farmer replied, 'Good thing? Bad thing? Who knows?'

A few days later, the horse returned from the hills and brought with him ten very fine horses.

The neighbours again gathered around. 'Oh, how lucky you are! Now you can do much more work than ever before! How lucky you are!' they said.

The farmer replied, 'Good thing? Bad thing? Who knows?'

Three weeks later, the farmer's son was bucked off one of the new horses and smashed his leg very badly.

'How unlucky!' exclaimed the neighbours.

The leg healed crookedly and left the son with a permanent limp and endless pain. The neighbours were concerned again.

'Now that he is incapacitated, he can't help you around the farm. And he will never find a woman who will marry him. What misfortune!'

The farmer replied, 'Good thing? Bad thing? Who knows?'

A few months later, the news came that a vicious war had broken out, and all the young men were conscripted to the army. The villagers were devastated because they knew that many of their young men would never come back. The farmer's son could not be drafted to the army because of his crooked leg.

The neighbours came to the old man again. 'How lucky you are! You get to keep your only son!'

The farmer replied, 'Good thing? Bad thing? Who knows?'

And on the story goes, forever.

Life will happen and continue evolving, regardless. What if you can alter your perception in the moment towards believing that there is a perfect reason for the way in which life is unfolding the way it is? Imagine how liberating it would be to live a life where we didn't label things as positive or negative.

Everything that seems on the surface to be bad may be good in disguise. And everything that seems good on the surface may not always be so.

One memorable situation for me was when I wanted to leave my job. I wanted to take a career break for a year so I would have a safety net to return to my job if things didn't work out. I was refused. Twice. Then I decided to take a big leap of faith and resign completely from my job, and on looking back, it was the best thing that could have happened. It gave me the impetus to make a huge change in my life. Resigning gave me the motivation to make things work in my new business. People took my work more seriously; I was not simply pursuing a hobby for a year and returning to my safe job. In so many ways that seemed crushing at the time, things actually turned out for the very best.

The thing was, the first time I was refused, I had done no work on building my resilience muscle and I was devastated, terribly upset. The second refusal was a lot easier to handle. I had begun the practice of resilience and could move past the setback quickly, smoothly and with ease. I did not let it get to me very much, which then allowed me to make the final decision of resigning from a clear and positive place.

Exercise

Good Thing, Bad Thing

- For one full day take note of each situation that happens to you. You will see how you immediately label them either good or bad. Become aware of how your mind is doing this.

- Think of events in your life that seemed good or bad at the time, and that later you could see from a different and changed perspective.

- 'Good thing, bad thing . . . who knows?' is a great quote to pin on your fridge, in your office, on the mirror in your bathroom.

Acceptance

The key to a resilient mindset is to understand that your feelings about a situation do not change the situation itself. Imagine you lose your job. You might feel angry, hurt, frustrated, and many other emotions. Those are all valid feelings, and you have a right to experience them – indeed it is good to experience them. But your anger will not undo the job loss. The job loss happened. The job loss simply is. Your emotional reactions are perfectly natural, and it is counter-intuitive to get worked up over what you 'should' be feeling. Note your feelings without judgement. Accept the situation and your feelings about it simply as they are. Doing this will help you resolve the issue in a more constructive manner.

Exercise

Acceptance

Below are examples of situations where you can practise acceptance. Of course you can add on more of your own personal situations too.

- The alarm clock fails to go off. You wake up later than planned.
- You are in the middle of cooking dinner and realise you are missing an ingredient.
- An unexpected bill comes in the post.
- The friend you were meeting does not turn up or even text.
- You didn't get the pay rise you expected at work.

Imagine if you could accept each of these situations as simply something outside your control – neither good or bad – and that you could train yourself to not get worked up over unexpected events. It is not an easy task but it is very worthwhile. It will take time to build the practice into your life. Be ever so gentle on yourself. Begin with the small stuff. You will take two steps forward and one step back and that is perfectly natural. In effect, you are re-wiring your brain and thought processes.

Life as learning

The more you can accept challenges in life as opportunities to advance and grow, the more resilient you will become. All of us experience pain at times, be it illness, disappointments at work, feeling let down by family or friends, losses or things not working out as we had expected. When you begin to see the learning opportunities offered in difficult situations, you will overcome the tendency to view them as insurmountable challenges and you will value the lessons and wisdom held within each experience.

What resilient people do is look at a situation and say, 'Is there a solution to that?' or 'What can I learn from it?' They are looking at pain as an opportunity to learn and problem-solve, and are building the confidence and the habit of dealing with an issue instead of running from it.

Exercise

Life as Learning

Think of a recent challenge or disappointment you have faced or are currently facing.

- How do you feel about it?
- Is there something you can do to improve this situation?
- What can you learn from this situation so that you can either avoid it happening again, or improve it in the future?

Your answers to these questions will empower you and will promote more expansive thinking and acceptance.

Connecting

Making connections and building your social support networks has been proven to strengthen resilience. When we have good familial, social or community support structures around us, it means we can ask and receive help and support from those who care about us. It's great to talk about problems with someone who will sincerely listen and give you time.

It can be equally beneficial to engage with those who have experienced similar challenges to yourself, as you can identify with them more. A knock-on result of this is that you will eventually be able to assist and support others, and you will feel wonderful for doing so. Being active in groups of like-minded people, volunteer groups or similar will provide great social support and hope.

> Being active in groups of like-minded people will provide great social support and hope.

Change

Accepting that change is a natural and unavoidable part of life will strengthen your resilience muscle. Without change life could not continue! Our lives are fuelled by change, though most of us want a certain amount of stability. There will be times in your life when there is more change happening than you might like or feel comfortable with. Acknowledging that things won't always change at such an excessive pace will be helpful in combating stress. If you can begin to accept change as a helpful friend rather than something to be avoided, you will experience less stress and more resilience.

Self-care

A regular routine of healthy habits – a balanced diet, good sleep and exercise – are fundamental to both mental and emotional resilience. You will then be much less likely to fall into unhealthy patterns following negative situations. Daily routines count. However, at times we all slip up, despite our best efforts. For example, if you've ever suffered from lack of sleep due to jet lag or a newborn baby you will understand just how fragile and reactionary it can make you. These things happen! Just acknowledge them and move on when you can.

Research shows that our brains are surprisingly active in moments when it seems like we are doing very little. MRI images of the brain at rest show that there is actually significant activity going on in the brain regions associated with decision-making, memories and the processing of emotionally significant events. Taking mental breaks and relaxation will help keep stress chemicals at bay, reducing the likelihood of becoming overwhelmed and reactive. It can be something as simple as setting a reminder on your phone each hour where you simply pause and breathe and become aware of your surroundings and thoughts. Regular meditation practice is also a wonderful way to relax. Please see the meditations to accompany this book at www.healingcreations.ie. Spending time outdoors in nature will also help combat anxiety and depression, improve immunity, and lower the levels of inflammatory chemicals in the body.

The subject of self-care will be looked at in more depth in Chapter 11.

An open heart

Being helpful to others is another powerful way of improving resilience. There are many studies in which researchers have found that serotonin, the neurotransmitter associated with feelings of happiness and well-being, is used more efficiently by people who engage in acts of kindness.

Once you add helpfulness and kindness to your life in a consistent way, the benefits become exponential, so that in times of difficulty you have a well of resilience to draw upon. There are great and fun ways to incorporate them into your life. I have some personal favourites:

* I often pay the toll for the car behind me at a toll booth. I ask the teller to let the driver behind know it's a random act of kindness and to pass it on to someone else.

* I don't have loyalty cards for most of the shops that I regularly use, so when I am at the checkout, I will ask the person behind me if they have a loyalty card and I give them my points.

* Another thing I like to do is make up the difference if I see someone is short of change at the till. It's pretty amazing how something this simple can brighten a person's day. Some people might look at you like you have ten heads, but now you are becoming resilient, so that doesn't matter!

Doing these small things can make you feel really good, and others too. Your serotonin is increased and so is theirs. It's a win-win situation for everyone.

It is worth saying that being open to receiving and appreciating kindness is just as important as offering it to others. This is because gratitude can also improve your resilience. There is a whole chapter about gratitude later in the book.

A good sense of humour

Laughing in the face of adversity can be profoundly healing, both for the body and the mind. Light-heartedness reduces tension to more moderate levels. Psychologically, choosing humour can be incredibly empowering. Playing with a situation makes a person even more powerful than sheer determination does. 'This is my toy; I am bigger than it. This doesn't scare me.'

Self-belief

Believing that you, rather than your life circumstances, impact your successes is another key factor in being resilient. The very fact that you are reading this book and doing this work means you already believe you have the power to create your own reality. When we perceive the ball to be in our court, we stress less and perform better. Our psychological well-being and work performance is also improved.

Now that you understand resilience is a muscle you train in order for it to get stronger, try out the exercises in the chapter in your daily life. As you work first on the smaller and less significant areas of your life, you will naturally begin to bring your new knowledge into bigger areas. So when faced with a serious matter like a relationship break-up, an illness or a bereavement, your stock of resilience will be there, ready to sustain, comfort and restore your balance and equilibrium.

Summary

- Resilience is not about being unaffected by stress or pressure; it is about recognising when and how you are affected by it and having at hand a toolbox of coping strategies.

- A resilient person lets negative feelings sit side by side with other thoughts and feelings. At the same time they are feeling, 'I'm upset about this', they are also thinking, 'but I'm grateful about that'.

- When you don't label something a good or bad thing, you don't suffer. Rather than encouraging us to decide whether something is good or bad, radical acceptance encourages us to simply accept things as they are.

- When you begin to see the learning opportunities offered in difficult situations, you will overcome the tendency to view them as insurmountable challenges and you will value the lessons and wisdom held within each experience.

- Making connections and building your social support networks has been proven to strengthen resilience.

- If you can begin to accept change as a helpful friend rather than something to be avoided, you will experience less stress and more resilience.

- A regular routine of healthy habits – a balanced diet, good sleep and exercise – are fundamental to both mental and emotional resilience.

- Laughing in the face of adversity can be profoundly healing, both for the body and the mind.

- Believing that you, rather than your life circumstances, impact your successes is another key factor in being resilient.

CHAPTER 7

Overcoming Negative Thinking

My life has been full of terrible misfortunes,
most of which never happened.
MICHEL DE MONTAIGNE

Negative thinking can take many forms. You can imagine or expect that bad things are going to happen to you, worry that your partner is going to leave, that your health is going to fail, that your car is going to break down, or that your career will come to a standstill and you will never move forward. You can worry about all of these things even though there is little or no evidence that any of them will happen in the future.

Negative thinking can hinder our brain's ability to deal with important tasks, preventing us from thinking clearly or processing information properly. Because negativity causes stress, it can affect the body physically, sometimes resulting in illness or emotional dysfunction.

I have heard people criticise the recent positive thinking movement by proclaiming themselves realists. But a realist is a person who accepts a situation as it is and who is prepared to deal with it accordingly. A realist does not envisage constant problems, compounding them by dwelling on how things can only get worse. A realist will think through a challenging situation strategically and find a workable solution. It is absolutely natural to have negative thoughts now and again, but we suffer if we have them consistently. If a negative thought is not useful to us in some way, then it is a waste of energy.

Positive versus negative

You may have heard this old story illustrating the difference between positive and negative thinking:

> Many years ago two saleswomen were sent by an English shoe manufacturer to Africa to investigate and report back on the market potential there. The first saleswoman reported back, 'There is no potential here – nobody wears shoes.' The second saleswoman reported back, 'There is massive potential here – nobody wears shoes.'

This provides one of the best examples of how a single situation can be viewed in two very different ways. We can either see the situation's problems and disadvantages, or we can focus on its opportunities and benefits.

Creating a new path with neuroplasticity

People default to either one way of thinking or the other: the glass is either half full or half empty. If you veer on the negative side of the thinking equation, never fear, because our default mode of thinking can be changed. We can rewire our brains so that we begin to see the positive instead of the negative. Our brains are constantly being moulded by experience. There is no denying that we all have very different thoughts and behaviours to those we had twenty years ago. This transformation is the concept of neuroplasticity in action, that our brain changes as we experience, learn, and adapt.

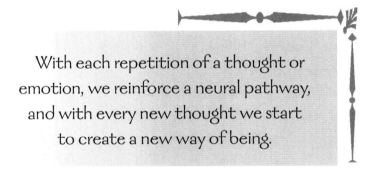

With each repetition of a thought or emotion, we reinforce a neural pathway, and with every new thought we start to create a new way of being.

Small changes frequently repeated lead to changes in our brain. Think of your brain like a field of grass that you walk across each day. Your thoughts cut across the grass of your brain, creating a pathway that gets more pronounced the more often you walk it. However, if you choose to start a path in a different area of the field – a path of new thoughts – and you keep walking that pathway daily, soon the old pathway will be covered up with grass and the new pathway will be the one that you automatically take.

Neuroplasticity is akin to the 'muscle building' part of our brain; we become better at the things that we do more often, while the things we do with less frequency fade away over time. Think of a musician. She practises and practises her instrument until it becomes natural to her. She corrects mistakes rather than repeating them over and over. That is how she achieves excellence. This is the physical basis of why repeating and refining thoughts increase their power. And in time, the thought or action becomes automatic. We literally become what we think and do with regularity.

Neuroplasticity is always at work throughout our lives. Connections within our brains are continuously changing, depending on what we are doing or thinking.

Notice your thoughts

The key to having the capacity to change your thought patterns from default negative to default positive is to become aware of the thoughts you are currently having. If you don't know your thoughts, how can you change them? Keeping a journal is a wonderful exercise. When you are writing, as well as noticing the negative thoughts you need to address, also acknowledge your positive self-talk, no matter how infrequent. Which thoughts leave you feeling uplifted, energised and looking forward to the future?

Now think of a busy street in a city. There are two people walking down the same street at the same time on the same day. At the end of their trip down the street they are asked what they noticed. The first person says: 'The traffic was chaotic and there was so much litter. The bins were literally overflowing and the place was too crowded. And the prices of the clothes in the department store – ridiculous!' The second person says: 'It was great to see so many people about on such a lovely day. There was a man feeding pigeons and they were landing on his shoulders and head and on the nearby statue. I could have watched them all day. Oh, and there was a brilliant sale on in the department store, a two-for-one offer on beautiful scarves. I'm going to buy one for myself and another for my friend.'

Same street, same time, same day. Two different mindsets. Your world is shaped by what you notice.

It can be difficult to keep track of all of our thoughts. It may be an idea to ask a friend or partner point out (in a friendly way!) the times when you are complaining or focusing on the negative, and also when you are lit up by the positive. I remember we had a swear box in our office. When someone cursed, another person would say 'beep' and that person would have to put a euro in the box. Some people ended up pretty broke by the end of the week, but gained huge awareness as to the amount of times they were cursing out loud. It proved to be a very useful exercise in awareness. So make a game of it – a 'bing' for positive and a 'beep' for negative!

Each morning, make a resolve to notice the good in your day. Pin on your mirror or wall: 'What do I choose to notice today?'

The Law of Momentum

Thoughts tend to gather momentum. If you find yourself spinning down a spiral of negative thoughts, it is important to pause and take note of what is happening. When a train is running in one direction, it has to stop before it can go in the opposite direction. It is a law of physics. It is the very same with our thoughts. You must give yourself the space to stop your train of negative thoughts.

A good way to help yourself is by doing a meditation, taking a nap or going for a walk. Only then try to focus on something more positive and you will begin to gain a healthier perspective on the situation that was causing the negative spiral. Of course positive thoughts also gain momentum, and that force will get stronger as you work on the practices held in this chapter.

Criticism

We can often find ourselves focusing on our perceived weaknesses and flaws, which can result in low self-esteem and a lack of confidence. Relentlessly mulling over mistakes you may have made in the past or about your physical appearance creates negativity. It would be useful to write about this in your journaling practice. Of course there is nothing negative about simply reflecting on past experiences – in fact, it can be extremely helpful if you reflect with the intention of learning from your mistakes or choices. But beating yourself up and wishing things were different, without making an effort to either change or accept them, is a fruitless task.

When you hear your inner talk running on a course of self-criticism, ask yourself, 'Would I speak to a friend or acquaintance this way?'

Then question yourself: 'Why am I speaking to myself this way?' Try to become more compassionate towards yourself. You can do this by noticing the things that you have accomplished and through gratitude practices (see Chapter 8). If you are being critical of your body or appearance, first of all, give thanks for the parts of your body that you love. Then ask yourself, 'Is there anything I can do about the parts I don't like?' Would some exercise or diet sort it out? If it is something that cannot be changed, moving towards acceptance of that fact is a healthy thing to do. If you feel you cannot accept this facet of yourself, getting counselling from a professional that you resonate with can be very helpful.

Similarly, if you find your inner mental chatter criticising other people or things with regularity, stop yourself for a moment. Have you slipped into bad habits? Say you go to a party, do you notice that the wine glasses don't match or do you notice how beautifully the room has been decorated? Do you notice how badly dressed some of the women are, or do you notice the warmth and exuberance with which the hostess greets you? When you find yourself in critical mode about others, ask yourself: 'Is there something good that I can see about this person or situation?'

Perhaps there is a person against whom you hold a grudge. You might find yourself thinking about them and what they have done to you. Forgiving yourself and others for past and current experiences is a powerful and liberating thing to do. We will cover forgiveness fully in Chapter 9.

Being critical of others can make for entertaining conversation. For many groups of people, it can actually be the default mode of conversation. Become aware of the conversations that happen in the different groups in your life: family, work or friends. Are these conversations uplifting and positive, or are they complaining, negative and gossipy? Try to observe the conversations that are happening around you as though you are outside them, and then ask yourself if these conversations are helpful. Motivational speaker Jim Rohn famously said, 'You are the average of the five people you spend the most time with.'

So be discerning. If you find yourself amid negative groups, try to gently change the topic of conversation and if this does not work, cut down on your time in this company.

> Motivational speaker Jim Rohn famously said, 'You are the average of the five people you spend the most time with.'

Don't judge yourself or others for this behaviour. It is natural for us to default into these habits. Our brains are hardwired to find the negative – that is what keeps us safe. From our earliest beginnings, being aware of and avoiding danger has been a critical survival skill. Complaining and gossiping can allow us to feel included in a group. We can bond through our disharmonious feelings about the world and others. However, you will most certainly find groups of people with whom you can bond equally well if not better by focusing on the positive and uplifting things in the world.

What if?

You may sometimes find yourself focusing on the lack of things in your life or on bad things in the world. You might believe that nothing can possibly change or get better. Your mind can catapult itself into a false future, conjuring up many 'what if' scenarios. For example, you are going for a job interview. Your mind begins to think ahead: What if my car breaks down on the way? What if I get sweat stains under my arms? What if everybody else being interviewed is brilliant and I make a mess of it?

If you find yourself doing this regularly, you have become trapped in negative thought patterning. When journaling, keep this aspect in mind. Notice where you are focusing on what is wrong or what could go wrong rather than on what is right or what could go right. Gratitude practices are wonderful in assisting us flip this type of thought patterning, so much so that the next chapter is devoted entirely to it.

Watching and listening to news all the time can leave us feeling hopeless and in fear that the world is falling apart. It is understood that we are hardwired to focus on the negative and so that is what is given to us. It sells more advertising and keeps us watching. News loops leave us drained and seeing the world as a fearful place. We hear about rapes and murders, and we fear: what if something bad happens to me or someone I love? Or we see wars and disasters and feel powerless, that there's nothing we can do to help. Harvard psychologist Steven Pinker speaks about this:

> Contrary to the impression that you might get from the newspapers – that we're living in a time of epidemics and war

and crime – the curves show that humanity has been getting better, that we're living longer, we are fighting fewer wars, and fewer people are being killed in the wars. Our rate of homicide is down. Violence against women is down. More children are going to school, girls included. More of the world is literate. We have more leisure time than our ancestors did. Diseases are being decimated. Famines are becoming rarer, so virtually anything that you could measure that you'd want to call human well-being has improved over the last two centuries, [and especially] over the last couple of decades.

Of course you want to be aware of what is happening in your country and in the world, but relentlessly watching, listening to or reading news can really bring us down. Keep news to a minimum. You are constantly being brainwashed by what is around you, so why not make a conscious choice on what you want to watch, read and listen to? There is no shortage of information available on the Internet, TV and radio that is positive, educational, enlightening and inspiring.

Limiting beliefs: identifying them

When you are noticing your negative thoughts, you will come across times when you make some broad and sweeping statements, for example: 'I'll never succeed in my career.' Now ask yourself, 'What is the evidence that I will never succeed in my career?' You might say, 'Well, there's this example of failure and that example of success.' How does that add up to *never*?

When we make blanket statements, it can be an indication of a deeply-held limiting belief. Limiting beliefs are stories that hold us back in some way from becoming all that we can be or want to be. They can often be unconscious, and we simply trot them out without even thinking. They are an acceptance of something being true without any actual proof. Holding them without question can keep you from making different choices in your life or from seeing opportunities and potential afforded to you. Limiting beliefs can be general or specific.

Some examples of blanket statements/limiting beliefs are:

* I could never do that because . . .
* They'll judge me if . . .
* I can trust no one because . . .
* I am a victim of my circumstances.
* Money is hard to earn.
* I am not (tall, small, thin, pretty, clever, confident, creative) enough.
* I don't have enough (time, support, money, experience).
* That's just the way I am.

Imagine you believe that you can trust nobody. Your belief will act like a lens through which you see everything. You will be constantly on the lookout for evidence that supports the 'fact' that the world is full of untrustworthy people, because your brain is wired to prove your belief. Usually these beliefs are held due to something that happened to you in the past. Say that you gave a customer credit, with the agreement that she would pay you next month. But she never did. You were devastated and angered, and so you decided that giving credit to customers was a bad thing. In one fell swoop you have lost your trust in everybody in the business world. You have set yourself up with a limiting belief based on one negative instance. Furthermore, you may have cut yourself off from possible future business opportunities.

Have you ever been about to buy a new car, and you are looking for a particular model? You have never really cared that much about cars before, but now, you are invested in buying one. Suddenly, this car seems to be everywhere. It's parked in front of your home. Your friend's husband has one. You see two of them in front of you in traffic on your way home from work. The car is even popping up in commercials on radio, TV, social media and magazines! So what exactly is happening here? Did this particular car suddenly come to dominate the social and cultural consciousness? Or is your mind playing tricks on you?

This is known as the Baader-Meinhof phenomenon. The phenomenon occurs when the thing that you have been focusing on suddenly crops up constantly. It gives you the feeling that out of nowhere, pretty much everyone is talking about the subject. You are not going crazy; you *are* in fact seeing it more. It is because you're noticing it more. The very same phenomenon is happening with your deeply-held limiting beliefs. If you believe that you can't trust people, you will notice many untrustworthy people.

Let's say you believe that people are good-natured, kind and trustworthy. This belief will then become the lens through which you view interactions and relationships. Your brain will be on the lookout for evidence to support this belief. And so, this is the kind of reality you will be more likely to experience.

With both beliefs, the people you interact with might not be any different. But what will be different is the way that you interpret their behaviour. It doesn't mean that you can simply say to yourself, 'People are trustworthy', and they will magically become that. That would not be a belief. That would be wishful thinking! But by holding this more positive belief, your experience of the world will radically shift. Ralph Waldo Emerson put it well when he said, 'To different minds, the same world is a hell and a heaven.'

Limiting beliefs: How to deal with them

Limiting beliefs can be tricky to spot. Why not try out some detective work by going back over your journal to see if you can spot evidence of one or more of these blanket statements that have no actual proof. We all have limiting beliefs, and uncovering them and bringing them into awareness is powerful.

Look out for statements such as, 'I can't start a new business/enter a new relationship/travel on my own because . . .' Once you become aware of your limiting beliefs, you can question them and begin to create and cultivate a more empowering belief that supports your growth. You can start to tell yourself a better story. In order to work through the limiting beliefs you uncover, it is helpful to identify how they originally found their way into your life. Ask yourself: 'How did I come to form this particular limiting belief?' and, 'What has made me hold onto it for so long?'

For a belief to change, your perspective and mindset needs to shift. To move forward it is important to determine what you are actually gaining by holding onto each of your limiting beliefs. To replace your limiting belief with a more empowering one, you will need to convince yourself that the value you're getting from this limiting belief is no longer needed.

Below is a questionnaire featuring examples of limited beliefs. After you read them do the questionnaire yourself, adding your own limiting beliefs, and see what answers come up for you. Make a game of it.

Questionnaire

Limiting Beliefs

1) INITIAL SELF-QUERY
The belief is: Money is hard to earn.

Q. What pleasure do I get from holding on to this belief?

A. I enjoy having the 'money is difficult' conversations with my friends – it bonds us. We talk about it a lot.

Q. Does this belief protect me from anything?

A. This belief keeps me 'safe' from moving forward with my dreams, and from facing possible rejection from my friends. (See Chapter 5: Making Friends with Fear)

Q. What can I do?

A. I must realise I do not have to believe what they believe in order to be friends with them. I will make efforts to have conversations about other interesting topics. That will be good for all of us! I will also look at my fear of moving forward.

In overcoming limiting beliefs, you must be certain in your mind that you are responsible for changing the belief. Change only happens when you are committed to moving forward.

Let's move on. You are now going to throw doubts upon a limiting belief from many different angles.

2) GOING DEEPER

The belief is: I can trust no one.

- Is this belief really accurate?

- Did I always believe this? Why?

- Was there a time when I did not believe this? Why didn't I?

- Are there times in my life when this belief simply doesn't make sense?

- Is there any evidence that disproves my belief?

- What would the exact opposite way of thinking about this belief be?

- How is this helpful?

- What is funny about this belief?
- What is odd about this belief?
- Is this belief helping me achieve what I want most in life?
- How does the opposite of what I believe work for other people?
- Are there common quotes or sayings that throw doubt upon this limiting belief?

These questions are designed to help you expand your perspective and see the possibilities of your situation. They will also help you to create new neural pathways towards a more empowering belief.

By bringing your conscious focus to your thinking patterns, you invite in a new awareness – mindfulness. You are able to step back from your thoughts and become the observer. In this way, thoughts and emotions start to lose their hold over you. It's not that you don't think or feel any more; it's simply that destructive thoughts no longer touch the essence of your being or shut you down in the same way. You become like a deep ocean, less affected by the waves on the surface. In time and with practice, your life will be transformed from the inside out.

Summary

- We often worry about things even though there is little or no evidence that any of them will happen in the future.
- With each repetition of a thought or emotion, we reinforce a neural pathway and with every new thought we start to create a new way of being.
- The key to having the capacity to change your thought patterns from default negative to default positive is to become aware of the thoughts you are currently having.
- If you find yourself spinning down a spiral of negative thoughts, it is important to pause and take note of what is happening.
- We can often find ourselves focusing on our perceived weaknesses and flaws. Try to be more compassionate towards yourself.
- Our minds can catapult themselves into a false future, conjuring up many 'what if' negative scenarios. Be discerning, and choose to focus on the positive.
- When we make blanket statements, it can be an indication of a deeply-held limiting belief. For a belief to change, your perspective and mindset needs to shift. It is important to determine what you are actually gaining by holding onto each of your limiting beliefs.
- By bringing your conscious focus to your thinking patterns, you will become mindful and able to deal with destructive thoughts in a balanced and harmonious way.

CHAPTER 8

Gratitude – The Gift that Keeps on Giving

You say grace before meals. All right.
But I say grace before the concert and the opera, and grace before
the play and pantomime, and grace before I open a book, and grace
before sketching, painting, swimming, fencing, boxing, walking, playing,
dancing, and grace before I dip the pen in the ink.

G.K. CHESTERTON

The attitude of gratitude – we've all heard about it. But does it really work? Studies over the past decade have shown that people who consciously count their blessings and show appreciation tend to be happier than those who do not. When I look back on difficult events that happened in my own life – divorce, having to sell the family home and more – I can now see what a gift it has been and I feel enormous gratitude for those experiences and all that I have learned from them. While they were happening, of course I did not like it one bit. It was immensely difficult. But it was during that period that I rediscovered my artistic gifts, began my journey of personal development, healing and growth, and ultimately arrived at what I do now for a living.

On some occasions we have to work harder than usual to find the positive and unearth its gifts. Sometimes those gifts only become apparent in retrospect, as they did for me in the example above. Now when something 'bad' happens, I can bring the notion of 'good thing, bad thing, who knows?' (see p. 72) to any problem I might face. I also look for lessons gleaned and am very grateful for them. I recall during that difficult time of solicitors, banks, running from appointment to appointment and not seeming to have a moment's peace, I would sometimes stop and look up at the sky or at a tree and appreciate its beauty. I was so thankful for these moments before I had to enter yet another office and fill out yet another form.

When you are in intense periods of upheaval like the one I was in, even these tiny practices of gratitude will go a long way in helping you cope.

Cultivating the habit of gratitude is a skill that we can profit from enormously by learning and practising it. Being grateful is the opposite of being discontented. It is about expressing appreciation for all that we have in our lives, however little that might be. It stops us being attached to what we want in the future, and prevents us from being miserable about something out there that is not yet ours. Gratitude and appreciation turns what we have into enough. There is always something to be grateful for no matter how desperate things might seem.

Life thankfully returned to normal for me but I kept up the practice of gratitude and I must say it makes for a much happier life. Gratitude changes your perspective and brushes away the petty day-to-day annoyances on which you focus so much of your attention. As you practise, you will find that you won't sweat the small stuff so much any more. Practising gratitude also rids you of self-pitying tendencies and self-centredness, while substantially increasing feelings of well-being and positive associations with others.

No matter what your situation, gratitude will help. It will always bring you to a higher place. You will become more content and satisfied with your life and situations. Your mood will improve as it gives you feelings of joy, optimism, pleasure and enthusiasm. Even your physical health can improve. Gratitude can help to lower your blood pressure, strengthen your immune system, and can make you feel less bothered about general aches and pains. Your sleep improves and you will find that you worry way less – always a good thing!

> Gratitude substantially increases feelings of well-being and positive associations with others.

Even your relationships can become enhanced by gratitude as it makes you feel more connected to friends, family and intimate relationships. Your spirit of generosity is increased, because grateful people are generally more helpful and better at 'paying it forward'. Your sense of compassion and empathy is increased and this of course will spill over to others in your life. Sounds pretty good, doesn't it? So how can you cultivate this amazing and life-changing habit?

What have the Romans ever done for us?

Roman Emperor and Stoic philosopher Marcus Aurelius wrote a famous book entitled *Meditations*. He began the book by naming all the people in his life, what he admired most about them and what he had learned from them. When I read the book, I loved that chapter and thought it was a really a beautiful and powerful thing to do. I tried it for myself, and saw how useful and beneficial this attitude was. Now you try!

Exercise

Gratitude for People in Your Life

Begin by taking a few moments to tune into your current mood and emotions.

* Identify between five and ten people in your life for whom you are grateful. Write down the reasons for your gratitude for these people. What qualities to you admire most in them? What have you learned from them? What are the best qualities in them that you would like to imbue into your own life?

When you are finished this exercise you may notice that you feel a little lighter and more positive.

The Stoics knew that wanting less leads to increased gratitude, just as wanting more obliterates it. They sought to reduce the destructive habit of always wanting more than they had. Constantly yearning for more is a way of life that we are very much encouraged to pursue in the Western world today. We are bombarded with messages of how we should have this and that to make us a more successful or beautiful woman. In practising gratitude and wanting less, the Stoics saw the key to a happy life and relationships. It is an old philosophy, but a wise one. It is okay and perfectly natural to want more, but it is also important to be happy with what you have in the now. Why not experience your happiness right now? Be grateful for the moment in which you are. You will then find that the universe opens its arms to you and what you want to manifest in the world will come to you more easily, whether that is love, money or friendship.

Evening Gratitude Meditation

Each evening before bed, make a list of all the things that you were grateful for in your day. I am not talking about a practical checklist, where you simply affirm that you have a roof over your head, or that you enjoyed a nice cup of coffee that morning. Instead, re-experience your events and as you do, express deep feelings of gratitude with all your senses.

For example, remembering your cup of coffee, really feel the cup in your hand and be grateful you can afford this delicious and reviving drink. Smell the beautiful aroma and feel its warmth as it goes down your throat. Recall the pleasure of each sip and give thanks again. Ooze appreciation of this moment from every pore of your body.

You may find it a little difficult to visualise this to begin with, but with practice it can be summoned at will. You will be learning more about creative visualisation later in the book.

I have also created a powerful guided meditation, available on www. healingcreations.ie, to assist you in embodying the feeling of gratitude within every cell of your body.

Journaling

Having a journal solely related to practising gratitude is a wonderful endeavour. Here are some ideas that can get you started. Remember, the world is your oyster, and the only limit is your imagination.

Exercise

Gratitude Journaling

* Identify three things that you feel grateful for and appreciate in your life. These things could be from the past, present or the future. There is no thing too big or small to appreciate, but do try to be as specific as you can.
* Next, find three things that you take for granted but that you are actually very thankful for. Everybody has things that they take for granted. Take the time to reflect and discover which of these you value the most.
* Now identify three things that you like and appreciate about yourself. Pick things that are meaningful. They can be related to your personality, your qualities, your actions, or anything else directly related to yourself.

> * Look at three things that you feel true appreciation for right now in this moment, as you are actually journaling. You might think about your environment, the time you're taking for your own well-being, or the chair or sofa beneath you. Literally anything that relates to the now.

The whole point of these exercises is to feel it within. Pick out one of the points above that really stand out for you. Now pause and breathe into it. Allow the warmth, love, appreciation, and gratitude to wash over you in waves. Don't worry if tears come; they are a perfectly natural reaction when you truly feel and embody gratitude.

Gratitude Jar

Another great exercise is to make a gratitude jar. The whole family can do this. I have done it with my daughter and it is quite amazing to see the results and watch her happiness increase too.

Get a nice big container. You could recycle an old jar or box or buy a new one, whichever you prefer. Every evening either alone or together, each person writes one thing from their day that they are grateful for on a small piece of paper. Date it, fold it and place it in the jar. Let the gratitude notes increase until the jar is full, and open it then – or wait until a special date for a 'grand opening'.

My daughter and I like to put notes into the jar all year and then open it on New Year's Eve. We sit together and read back our moments of gratitude from the whole year. It brings back beautiful memories, appreciation and so much gratitude and is a really beautiful energy in which to bring in the new year.

These simple practices will increase your feelings of gratitude. And those feelings not only improve your relationships, but also bring more love and appreciation into your daily life.

Feeling gratitude for the success of others

The Stoics believed that we should seek the success of our friends and peers with as much fervour as we put into manifesting our own success. Seneca put it this way:

> It is in keeping with Nature to show our friends affection and to celebrate their advancement, as if it were our very own. For if we don't do this, virtue, which is strengthened only by exercising our perceptions, will no longer endure in us.
>
> Seneca, Moral Letters, 109.15

If you are prone to feeling jealousy at other people's successes, it would be good to question yourself about it. It is quite likely that you want to have or do something the other person owns or has done. What is it? Why can you not have it? The feeling reveals nothing about the other person but shines a light on you. What does their success reveal about your own desires? Is there a limiting belief within you as to why you couldn't achieve the same or more? What actions can you take to move forward in the way that you want in your own life?

All of these feelings are gifts, enabling us to learn more about how we operate in the world, as well as showing us where we want to go. Jealousy is like taking a wrong turn or coming across the obstacle of a limiting belief. Your internal GPS system (see p. 23) gives you the jealous sensation, but also the opportunity for you to learn and grow, thereby getting you back on track.

A few years ago, I became a member of a wonderful online community called 'Bite the Biscuit'. It is a community for creatives to learn, share their work, get advice from each other, support each other, network and so much more. The energy of this group is quite amazing. Collaborations happen. People help each other with no expectation of return.

> When you come together in a supportive way, you discover that your subconscious mind begins to change your own default critic.

There are people ahead of you on their creative journey from whom you can learn, and people behind you whom you can help. Successes are celebrated openly without jealousy or envy. If people do experience envy or feel less than they should about their work, they can voice it. People will then help them to overcome the limitation of that emotion and see the learning and value held within it. Through this practice, they become genuinely happy for the successes of others and that is a liberating and powerful thing.

Find a group of supportive people in your field who truly get what you do. If you can't find one, either in the physical world or online, why not create one yourself? There is enormous power in a supportive community, as already mentioned in the chapter on resilience. When you come together in an encouraging and helpful way, happy to celebrate the successes of others, you will discover that your subconscious mind begins to change your own default negative critic. You become able to affirm in your own minds that you too deserve success.

Realise that the success of others in your life is not at your expense but to your benefit. By releasing envy and jealousy, you receive freedom from frustration and worry and you have more energy to focus positively on where you want to go.

Summary

- Studies have shown that people who consciously count their blessings and show appreciation tend to be happier than those who do not.

- Practising gratitude rids us of self-pitying tendencies and self-centredness, while substantially increasing feelings of well-being and positive associations with others.

- Gratitude can help to lower your blood pressure, strengthen your immune system, and can make you feel less bothered about general aches and pains.

- Roman Emperor and Stoic philosopher Marcus Aurelius

wrote a famous book entitled *Meditations*. He began the book by naming all the people in his life, what he admired most about them and what he had learned from them.

- Every evening make a list of all the things you were grateful for that day.

- Create a gratitude journal.

- Get the family involved in putting gratitude notes into a gratitude jar, to be opened and read out at a specific date.

- Let other people's successes ignite hope in you for the successes that will soon be coming your way!

CHAPTER 9

Reclaiming Freedom through Forgiveness

*To forgive is to set a prisoner free
and discover that the prisoner was you.*
LEWIS B. SMEDES

For many of us, forgiveness can be one of the most difficult things to do. Reactions to being wronged vary from person to person: some try to solve the issue; some people are neutral, perhaps becoming numb to the event; and others may find it extremely difficult to move on.

Holding onto a grudge can become all-consuming, affecting our minds and bodies. We go over and over a situation where we feel a real or perceived wrong was done to us. We wage battle in our heads with this enemy. But the enemy isn't in our heads. We are. So in effect, we wage battle with ourselves. When we do this, we give away our energy to the person whom we perceived has wronged us.

It can stop us moving forward with our lives. Also, blaming another for our own 'stuckness' can provide us with an excuse for not progressing. If this arises for you, revisit Chapter 5: Making Friends with Fear.

I once knew a man, let's call him Aidan, who held a grudge against a co-worker. Every day, the conversation would inevitably turn to this man and what he had done or was currently doing. Fifteen years later the man passed away, but even after his death Aidan held onto his grudge. It is pretty phenomenal how resentment can nestle and loop relentlessly inside people's minds. I am sure that if Aidan had known better he would not have wasted his time or energy on this person.

Forgiveness is a Choice

Forgiveness is a choice that only you can make. Becoming conscious of your thoughts is the first step that needs to happen. Taking moments throughout your day to check in with your thoughts or by journaling is a great way to gain awareness of your inner dialogue. Acknowledge your thoughts of resentment or grievance without judgement and take note of how much of your time and energy these thoughts consume. Remember that sometimes the wrong is most definitely wrong, and other times it is just a perception in your mind.

> Forgiveness transmutes anger and hurt into peace and healing.

We often think that to forgive is to condone what the other person has done. What if forgiveness was actually a mechanism to free you from an internal cycle of self-imposed suffering, and a way to gain freedom for yourself? Forgiveness transmutes anger and hurt into peace and healing. It can help overcome feelings of anxiety, rage and depression and will also help you in your relationships with others. It is about making a conscious decision to let go of a grudge. The power to release it lies with you. It is not about letting someone away with a wrongdoing and it definitely does not mean that you stay around for future mistreatment from a partner, parent, boss or friend.

Anne Lamott famously declared, 'Forgiveness is giving up all hope of having had a different past.' It is understanding that you cannot change the past, but that you have a choice of how you wish to proceed into the future. You cannot control others and what they choose to do or not do, but you can control your own choices. There will be people that you wish to forgive and that you never want in your life again and that is fine. Keep that boundary. There will be others you wish to forgive and with whom you want to maintain a relationship into the future.

True forgiveness versus half-hearted forgiveness

True forgiveness has two components: letting go and forgetting. However, some people may let go but they don't forget, and keep pondering and ruminating about the wrong that was done to them. They keep the grudge alive inside. It is like having a sore on your arm: if you keep at it and agitating it, it gets bigger and may become infected. Half-hearted forgiveness

If you truly forgive, you wipe the slate clean.

can lead to toxicity in your relationships in the future. But if you truly forgive, you wipe the slate clean. You allow the wound to fully heal. Forgiveness is choosing to compassionately release the desire to punish another for an offence.

When you half forgive and are holding on to and prodding the grudge inside, you are prone to self-righteousness. You are proud of yourself for having forgiven the other person. You're keeping a scorecard. One for me, nil for you. You've developed an air of superiority and are up on a pedestal in the relationship. And when the other person does something that bothers you or disturbs you, you can just 'give the look' or even pull the scorecard from your pocket and say, 'Remember this, remember I forgave you.'

Can you see the toxicity of this kind of forgiveness? You have forgiven the other person in name only. On the inside, you haven't really forgiven because you're always thinking about it. The slate has not been cleared.

When you forgive and want to maintain a relationship with the person involved, you can evidently see some good in this connection. Your conscious choice to forgive them is a pact between you and you, not between you and them. Yes, something wrong has happened, but you are making a promise to yourself to let go and to never think about or bring it up again. The other person has nothing to do with it. To truly forgive someone takes inner strength and courage but is absolutely worth it.

Forgiveness meditation

Below is a gentle and effective meditation on forgiveness. Find a time you can set aside without any distractions. Being alone in a safe space is recommended, but if you wish you can have someone you trust nearby.

Before you start:

* Make a list of every person, going right back to your childhood, who has done a wrong against you in some way. If the memory is active emotionally, it is still affecting you, even though you may not be fully conscious of it. When you finish your list, prioritise by putting the names in the order of who hurt you the least to those who hurt you the most. I would urge you to begin the practice of forgiveness with those small hurts, for example, forgiving the person who cut you off in traffic today, or a rude waiter in a restaurant.

* Each forgiveness meditation centres on just one person. Give yourself plenty of time to work through your list. It could take you days or weeks – whatever feels right for you.

* You will be focusing on forgiving the person rather than the action they have done. Let's say a person has stolen from you. The theft itself is morally wrong and would be hard to forgive as an act in and of itself. The person who stole from you, on the other hand, may be battling unknown hurts or be struggling in some way that drove them to steal.

* Please know that you are allowed to feel sad and angry. You have been hurt and your feelings are valid. Allow these feelings to surface. Observe them. Don't rush the process.

116

Meditation

Begin by sitting comfortably or lying down, whichever feels best for you. Take three deep breaths, in through the nose and out through the mouth.

Now bring to mind a person who has hurt you. Feel in your body where you are hurting. Imagine what colour the hurt is, what shape, what texture. Allow yourself to completely feel it as though it is happening right now.

During this forgiveness process and the meditation, it is normal to feel pain, sadness, anger and frustration. You might find tears coming. Allow them. If you feel anger, allow it to surface. Beating a pillow is a great way to release it.

Allow yourself to feel your emotions without judgement. These are natural, and feeling into them deeply will allow you to release them. Hard as it might be, doing this will ultimately allow you to move on.

Now the work on forgiveness begins. Think about the person in a new light. Were they hurt in any way either in this situation or in the past? If they were, did their hurt possibly contribute to your hurt? Acknowledge the other person's humanity.

If you can step into their shoes and come to understand their suffering, your heart can develop the conditions for forgiveness and growth. There is a great saying: 'Hurt people hurt people'.

In your mind's eye, see this person as a small child of perhaps three years of age. See yourself also as a small child. Recognise that you both have had life experiences that have led to this situation. Begin to feel your heart soften and feel compassion for this other child you see before you in your mind's eye.

Now ask: Did I hurt this person in some way? If so, feel compassion and forgiveness for yourself too. You have now reframed the situation in your mind. You are seeing more deeply into it.

Now it is time to surrender the grudge. Visualise a golden ball of light passing from your body into their body and from theirs to yours. Feel into your body and allow the light to expand and fill up the spaces where you felt the hurt.

Keep doing this until you feel lighter and relaxed and a calmness enfolding you. Again, bring your awareness to your breath, noticing your in breath and your out breath and how they happen with no effort. In, out, like the tide. Effortless. Then rest for a few moments.

Slowly and in your own time, stretch and open your eyes.

There is also a deep and very powerful forgiveness meditation to accompany this chapter on www.healingcreations.ie.

Self-care is vital during this process. Forgiveness can be a difficult but profoundly healing experience. Be extra kind to yourself as you do this work and do things that nourish you. Good rest, good food, good company and good sleep are vital. The last chapter of this book is entirely devoted to the important matter of self-care.

Sometimes, inadvertently, a story of hurt resurfaces and starts replaying in your mind, even though you had forgiven and let go. Stop and say to yourself, 'Success! I have caught myself.' Take three breaths into the stomach. Then say, 'These are simply thoughts. I am leaving this situation behind, I have made that choice.' And bring your attention to something else. Try not to judge yourself for having these thoughts; they are natural. Rather, give yourself a pat on the back for catching yourself and being willing to take back the reins of control on your thoughts. You can repeat the meditation with certain stubborn issues as often as necessary.

Take the time needed to process your emotions. You will know when it's time to move to the next person on your list. You will find that there is a reflection period involved when the pain passes. Journal your thoughts. You will come to realise that you have become stronger, and that you are happier and lighter. You will be able to move on with your life in a positive and productive manner.

And remember, when it comes forgiving someone who keeps hurting you, make sure you distinguish this from tolerating future emotional injuries. You can practise forgiveness and let go of grudges while still refusing to let a toxic person back into your life. In those cases, that may be what you need to do in order to attain well-being.

Self-Forgiveness

We have all done things in our lives we are not proud of. These things are held within us, blocking us and tormenting us. Perhaps there is something that you can do to make amends with a person you have wronged? A letter of apology is a very powerful thing to write, even if you never send it.

Think of the things you have done for which you need forgiveness and write them down. When we realise how much we need to be forgiven for the wrongs we have done, it makes it easier to forgive others who have hurt us. We all make mistakes in life. The meditation above can also be done to forgive yourself. Simply visualise the other person as you. Go easy on yourself. You are courageous to take the steps of forgiving both yourself and others.

As we expand our ideas about what forgiveness is, we begin to experience that forgiveness and healing are one and the same. Each time we release ourselves from grudges, hurts, guilts or fears, we are forgiving and healing ourselves from the adverse effects of our thoughts.

Summary

- Forgiveness can be one of the most difficult things to do. Reactions to being wronged vary from person to person.

- If you hold a grudge against someone for something they have done to you, the person who suffers most in the long run is you.

- Forgiveness is a mechanism that frees you from an internal cycle of self-imposed suffering, and a way to gain freedom for yourself.

- True forgiveness has two components: letting go and forgetting. Half-hearted forgiveness can lead to toxicity in your relationships in the future. If you truly forgive, you wipe the slate clean.

- Meditation is a powerful aid to healing and moving on in life.

- After a forgiveness meditation take the time needed to process your emotions. You will know when it's time to move on to the next person on your forgiveness list.

- We have all done things in our lives we are not proud of. Perhaps there is something that you can do to make amends with a person you have wronged.

- We all make mistakes in life. As we expand our ideas about what forgiveness is we learn that forgiveness and healing are one and the same.

CHAPTER 10

Creative Visualisation

Cherish your visions and your dreams as they are the children
of your soul, the blueprints of your ultimate achievements.
NAPOLEON HILL

You will have heard of many celebrities who have used the technique of creative visualisation, from Oprah Winfrey to Jim Carrey. In 1987 Carrey wrote himself a cheque for ten million dollars for acting services rendered, dated ten years into the future. He was a struggling actor at the time and would sit on the Hollywood hill in the evenings with this cheque tucked in his wallet, feeling and visualising what it would be like to be a successful actor. Before ten years had passed, he had succeeded in his goal.

I have found vision boards and creative visualisation meditations profoundly powerful. Many of the things that I have placed on my boards and in meditations have manifested in my life, and I have to say that I have enjoyed the journey of manifestation even more than the outcomes themselves! Creative visualisation techniques involve using your imagination to visualise specific future feelings, behaviours and events happening in your life. The idea is to create vivid and detailed imagery of what you desire and then visualise it over and over using all of your physical senses. For example, a musician visualises playing a piece over and over again to mentally train her muscle memory so she can play the tune perfectly in real life.

Visualisation methods help you invest the time and energy to visualise your future and will consistently remind you of how you want your life to feel, look and be. They keep your attention on your intentions.

Expectations

Before we get to working on your creative visualisation, it is useful to look at the concept of expectations. An extraordinarily liberating thing to bring into your life is the ability to live with a looser grip on expectations. When you have rigid expectations, you have developed preconceived ideas of how things should be and how and when they should happen. Then when things happen in a different way, or someone behaves in a way not in alignment with your expectations, you suffer disappointment and more.

When you become freer in your expectations, you can simply go with the flow of the universe. You can allow unexpected things to happen and in doing so, different avenues of potential suddenly open out before you. As a result, you are less affected by the outcomes that you encounter in your life. Trust that every outcome, whether you perceive it as good or bad (remember 'Good thing, bad thing . . . who knows?'

from Chapter 6), can serve to move you towards an even greater realisation of your desires. So do not worry if there are times when you may feel you are moving backwards. Keep faith in your desires and goals.

I hear you ask: Surely a chapter on creative visualisation involves having expectations? Well, yes and no. In my experience it is far better to focus on the feelings you wish to manifest in your life rather than on particular outcomes happening in fixed ways. So yes, you know the feelings you want to embody, and you set goals and expect to manifest them, but you stay very loose in the how, the who, the when or the where of them. It is about being open and surrendering as to how things might manifest, and in what form. That is the magic of creative visualisation.

> It is far better to focus on the feelings you wish to manifest in your life rather than particular outcomes happening in fixed ways.

Let me give you an example of this concept. I practise a form of art known as mandala art. It is a form of meditation in itself and the way I work is to allow the piece to flow intuitively. Sometimes these paintings are geometric and other times they are free-flowing. I begin with a simple dot and no idea in my head as to what the finished piece will look like. Not even the colours are thought out beforehand. The goal is to create a beautiful artwork and to be fully absorbed in the process. However, there is no attachment as to how it might look or how it might come about.

When I teach this art practice, this is the notion that people find most difficult to grasp. Many find it hard to let go of set expectations. There is an urge to plan ahead. But when people do embrace the process of letting go and allowing the artwork to unfold, magic happens on the page. The piece flows in directions that they could never have logically conceived.

Of course at times the brain will move some steps ahead in the process. Often I would think: Ooh, a red dot might look nice here or a blue line there. Then my pen might leak and the red dot becomes a blob that I didn't want. In the beginning this challenged me, but gradually I learned to accept it. And now when 'mistakes' happen in the work, I allow them to lead me. They bring me in directions that I would never have considered and sometimes these paintings end up being my best works.

I began to take this philosophy into my life. One morning as I was dropping my daughter to school, I closed the front door behind me and reached into my bag for the car keys. No keys. I looked up and saw them through the window sitting on the table. And I had no spares.

But, this time, instead of getting frustrated and having thoughts like, 'Poor me, why does this always happen to me!', I took three deep breaths. I decided that instead of getting frustrated and angry, I was going to get curious. I was going to let this 'mistake' lead in the same way that I allow in my artwork. I called a friend who collected my daughter for me and dropped her to school. Then I ambled into my neighbour who called a locksmith for me and put on the kettle for coffee. I remained very relaxed and curious. We chatted and out of that conversation came an opportunity for another project that I was working on.

I hadn't spent my time in my neighbour's house lamenting the hardship of the situation and getting him to agree with me on how awful it all was. I let it go. I simply didn't give it energy. My expected day of a smooth ride to school and a smooth return home to do some work had gone awry, but I let go of the expectation that I had woken up with and allowed what was actually happening to simply happen. The upshot of it all was that I thoroughly enjoyed the morning. Having an attitude of curiosity instead of struggle about what was happening was liberating.

Obviously we need to make plans for our day and indeed our lives. Setting goals is a wonderful habit and you will be setting goals for your vision board a little further on in this chapter. But when your goals are too tight and rigid, it is like making a beeline down a corridor full of open doors and heading for one particular door that you have fixed your mind on. You miss what is behind all of the other doors. You don't allow serendipity to work its magic.

Letting go of rigid expectations about when and how things manifest is freeing, and can lead you to even better things than you had ever envisaged, just as in the painting process described above. You are allowing your life to unfold and are co-creating with it, rather than directing the show in a fixed way and struggling when it doesn't happen that exact way. You will experience more moments of *kairos* that we spoke about in Chapter 4. You seem to be in the right place at the right time. You are open. You are in the moment. You are in flow. And most importantly, you are enjoying the dance of your life. There is no struggle. I believe this to be the key to successful creative visualisation.

In my vision boards and meditations, I tend to look forward in periods of three years. If we take one year, we tend to think we can do more than is realistically possible in that time, but three years seems to hit a sweet spot.

As you regularly focus with intent on the images on your vision board, or do creative visualisation meditations, allow yourself to completely trust that your desires will happen. In fact, invoke feelings that they already have!

> Of course action is needed, but when you are in flow your actions will be more guided and indeed more enjoyable.

This doesn't mean that you can lie back and meditate and all will appear before you. Of course action is needed, but when you are in flow your actions will become more guided and indeed more enjoyable. You will have a keener sense of the right thing to do, the right place to go and the right people to talk to. Your internal guidance system will operate in a clearer way.

Manifestation in Action

Let me give you an example of how a particular manifestation came about for me. For over two years, I had on my board an image of an artist's studio in an old courtyard in a beautiful place that was close to my home. I was very open as to where this desired studio might be. I was not attached to the place in any way other than it evoked feelings of peace and tranquillity, and it was easy to get to.

A few weeks after leaving my job, I was walking down the street, and had a chance meeting with a woman I know. We began chatting. 'Did you know,' she said, 'The old courtyard in the park is being renovated and I believe they are looking for submissions from artists.' Say what? I thought. Wow, that's interesting. I went home and did an Internet search and sure enough, the whole place had been beautifully restored and submissions were open for artists to apply for renting studio spaces. I sent off for the application and made an appointment to view the studios.

I put it in my diary, but completely forgot about it. One morning, after dropping my daughter to school, I felt poorly and thought of going back to bed. But suddenly a voice inside me (my internal GPS) said, 'Check your diary and make sure you've nothing on today.' And there it was: my viewing appointment was in half an hour's time! I smartened myself up quickly and headed for the park. There were ten viewings that day with approximately ten people at each viewing.

When I got there, I happened to meet a friend who co-owns a skin care business. She and her business partner are also members of a business group that I am a part of. She just happened to be on the very same viewing slot as me. We were brought around and simply loved the place. I knew the rent was pretty much out of my league. I did not get upset about it and thought to myself: 'Good thing, bad thing, who knows?' I trusted that it all would work out, perhaps at a different time and place.

My friend and I decided to go for coffee afterwards and whilst chatting, it turned out that the rent was out of both her and her partner's league too. But what if we went together and shared the space? And so it happened. We sent off our application as a joint venture. Had I become upset that the rent was too high for me, I might have gone home and not felt much like going for coffee. Do you see how being unattached and surrendering is very helpful?

We went for the interview to apply for the space, in which there were three people on the interview board, one of whom was from the National Museum of Ireland. I discovered that she had written a book on Asian art objects, including mandalas. Exactly the unusual art form that I do! There were so many moments of *kairos* – perfect opportune moments – surrounding that situation. Right people, right place, right time. Nudges from the universe and synchronicities were rife.

I believe that in letting go of exactly how I wanted my desired outcome to happen and being open to other avenues of how it might come about allowed that manifestation to happen. Had I been fixed on having my own studio and thinking that nothing else would do, I would have missed all of the opportunities being presented. It also meant that I could avail of my friend's experience in retail. It was something I had no experience of, and so all that I have learned from the partnership since then has been and continues to be invaluable.

Vision boards

Vision or dream boards are created from pictures, quotes, words, textures and can be made physically or digitally. Traditionally they have been done using pictures and quotes. I do feel that we can add more things to them, like sound, poetry, music and texture. The aim is to utterly stimulate your senses to feeling the essence of what you desire.

Knowing your personality type will really assist you in deciding what kind of vision board you wish to create. It is generally accepted that personalities fall into three different types:

- Visual (seeing/image)
- Auditory (hearing/sound)
- Kinaesthetic (feeling/touch)

When information reaches our brains, it is given meaning and forms our subjective experience of the world. Although we use all three of these systems, we usually have a preference of one over another. If you are not sure which personality is dominant in you, you can find out by accessing free online tests.

If you are a visual person like me, strong visual images will work for you. When gathering images, really play with your own perception of how you view the world. If you are auditory, saying, reading or hearing words and sayings may feel more powerful and meaningful. You might even play music or read poetry that evokes the right mood for you as you meditate on your board. For the kinaesthetic person, it's all about touch and feeling. Find images and words that embody the feeling of what you want. Say you want comfort and luxury, find images of cashmere or velvet; even use actual pieces of these materials so that you can physically touch them on your board.

You can create your board using physical materials or digitally on your computer, tablet or phone. Just make sure that it is easily accessible and that it resonates with your lifestyle. For example, if you live in a shared home or you travel a lot, you might want to have a more private board on your laptop or in a scrapbook. If you have a private space, like a bedroom or office area, then a physical board may suit better.

Take some time to really consider the message you want your vision board to convey and how you want it to look. What are the feelings, wishes and desires that you want to manifest? Think about your career goals, your love life, your family life, friendships, health and fitness, free time, holidays, spirituality, lifelong learning, finance, and more. Also think about how you would like your life to affect others. What benefits will you be bringing to the world? You can create a board for each aspect or create one big board for everything. It is entirely a personal choice. Personally, I use both Powerpoint and Pinterest for my boards and have different slides or boards for each section of life. Once you decide which kind of board you will use, follow the guidelines on the next page to create it.

Exercise

Creating Vision Boards

PHYSICAL VISION BOARD

- Obtain a board of the size and colour you prefer and that suits your space.
- Buy glue, scissors and tape.
- Attach images and words/sayings on it that resonate completely with you. These are images that evoke the feeling of what you want within every pore of your being! Make your board vibrant and attractive. Cut out things that inspire a positive or curious response from you. You can source images from:
  — Newspaper/magazine cutouts
  — Pages from books
  — Images/quotes printed from the Internet; Pinterest boards are especially recommended
    (Pinterest is a brilliant visual website and social network)
  — Photographs
  — Brochures/leaflets/flyers
  — Items from nature (feathers, leaves, shells etc.)
  — Fabric or jewellery
- Use glue and tape for photographs printed from the Internet and cut out from magazines. But if you are using precious

items or original photographs, get acid-free, removable adhesive.

Remember, this is not about creating an artistic masterpiece but creating something personal and inspiring. If you find that you have no idea where to start, simply start flicking through magazines and look for words, phrases or pictures that inspire you. You can of course draw or paint other details onto the board. Be as creative and as unconventional as you like!

When you have finished, put your vision board where you will see it every day to inspire, focus and remind you of your goals. Once in a while, take it down and look deeply at it. Review it and allow yourself to feel enthusiastic and excited. It can be great to put on some inspiring music or a guided meditation while you do this. Also, focusing on your board just before you go to bed is a great idea as your mind will automatically ponder and absorb it overnight.

ONLINE VISION BOARD

* Another great way to create your vision board is to create it on your computer using an application such as Word, Powerpoint, Pages or whatever software package is easiest for you.

* After you upload all your images, words and sayings to your digital board, you can save it as a PDF and have it available on your phone, so that you can take regular looks at it during

the day while you are waiting for an appointment or at break times.

* There are also many specialised apps for creating vision boards, meaning that you can have them with you on the go! You can have one overall slide, or separate slides for different areas of your life. Again, you can play music, poetry or guided meditations whilst focusing on your board to accentuate the process.

Review your board on a regular basis. I have kept slides of some of the manifestations that have already happened. I have printed a big 'MANIFESTED!' over these particular images. This gives me the memory that this process has worked for me in the past and will definitely work on even bigger dreams and goals. It allows me to connect with that positive vibe.

Creative visualisation meditation

In my own method of creative visualisation I have found creative visualisation meditation wonderful to do alongside focusing on a vision board. Some people might say, 'But I can't imagine things' or 'I can't really feel it or see it.' If that is the case, I'd like you to try a simple exercise. Close your eyes. Imagine you are holding a lemon in your hand. See yourself cutting the lemon into sections. Now imagine yourself putting a section of the lemon into your mouth and biting into it. Feel the juice squirting into your mouth and onto your tongue. Can you feel how your salivary glands have actually physically reacted?

So you see your imagination is powerful. You have the capacity to imagine and this capacity becomes better and better with practice.

Meditation

Creative visualisation meditation allows you to completely feel into what it is you want to achieve in life. I find that looking and feeling ahead into a day three years from now works very well. First of all, find a place where you will not be disturbed. Sit on a chair or lie down, whichever is most comfortable.

Become aware of your breath, noticing the in breath and the out breath and how they happen so easily. In, out, like the tide, effortless. Next, imagine a golden ball of light hovering above your head. See it intensifying, and filling with a nurturing light. Let that light pour down now through the top of your head, your forehead, face, neck, shoulders, heart, abdomen, hips, legs, feet. Feel each area of your body fill with this light, melting away any stresses or strains in your body.

In your mind's eye, visualise yourself in your kitchen three years from now. Is it the same kitchen you have now, or is it some place else? Look out the window. What can you see?

When you are ready draw your attention back to the kitchen.

Somewhere in the room you see a photograph of a recent holiday. Feel a smile form on your lips at the memory of this wonderful holiday and the people you shared it with.

Now move towards your fridge. Open the fridge door. What foods are inside? See them, smell them. Are the foods different, perhaps healthier? Take something fresh and sweet from the fridge and place it in your mouth. Taste it. Feel the saliva form in your mouth and the sensations of this wonderful flavour. Now close the fridge door.

Going back to the table, you notice your laptop or computer there. Sit down and turn on your computer and look at your emails. What do you see? Perhaps there is an email from a happy client in your new business or job. Open this email and read it. Feel deep satisfaction at the service you have been able to provide for this person. Also, feel how delighted the person is and feel grateful for the money that has been paid to you for that service or job. Smiling, you close the email.

You notice another email pop in. Open it. It is a confirmation email for your next wonderful trip away. Feel excitement well up inside at the thought of this trip and all you will see and learn.

After checking any other emails that catch your eye, close this program and open your online banking. What is the balance? See the number and feel happiness and safety radiate throughout your body. You also feel satisfied because you know that you have earned that money and that the people who paid you are happy. Gently close your laptop.

Rise from the chair and feel your bare feet on the floor. Walk from the kitchen towards your bedroom. Open the bedroom door and look around. Go to your wardrobe and open it. Run your hand along the fabrics of the beautiful clothes hanging up. You know that each garment expresses the true you. Feel great appreciation for having clothes that fit perfectly for your authentic lifestyle.

You have a wonderful event coming up this Friday evening and you are very much looking forward to it. What is the event? Now pick an outfit from your wardrobe that will be simply perfect. You will feel and look your very best in this. Lay the outfit out on your bed. Touch the material and notice the textures, the patterns, the colours. You smile at the thought of attending the event.

Now you turn and notice a small pile of books beside your bed. What are you reading? What new things are you learning? Sitting on the bedside locker is a framed photograph of the people that you love. Pick the photograph up and look at their faces. Feel love and gratitude well up inside you.

As you make your way back to the kitchen, you hear a car pull into the driveway. Hear the doors close and footsteps on the gravel or driveway. You hear the key in the door or the doorbell ring and in come the people that you love. Embrace them. Look deeply into their eyes. You see them smile at you, and you smile back. Feel utter gratitude for these loving relationships. Now look around your house one last time. Do you notice anything else?

When you are ready, sit down on a comfortable chair somewhere in your house and begin to notice your breathing again, feeling the in breath and the out breath.

Let your mind drift and become aware of your body in the present time, where you are sitting or lying. Listen to the sounds inside and outside the room.

Now, very slowly and in your own time, move your fingers and your toes and gently open your eyes.

As you can see, your mind has a great ability to create imagery, sensations, feelings and emotions. As you practise using your imagination in this way, these aspects will become stronger and more creative. I find it is very powerful to do this meditation either before or after gazing at your vision board, and as already recommended, bedtime is a good time to do both processes. Your hopes and desires, wishes and intentions will continue into your dream space, percolating in your subconscious mind overnight.

A deep recorded guided meditation for creative visualisation is available at www.healingcreations.ie. This meditation is similar to the meditation above, where you experience a day in your life three years from now. Being guided keeps your attention on the meditation and will also help to put aside any scepticism or worries you may have about doing it right.

Albert Einstein said, 'Imagination is more important than knowledge. For knowledge is limited to all we now know and understand, while imagination embraces the entire world, and all there ever will be to know and understand.'

Creative visualisation is a fun and playful process. Enjoy it!

Summary

- Creative visualisation techniques involve using your imagination to visualise specific future feelings, behaviours and events happening in your life.

- Visualisation methods keep your attention on your intentions.

- An extraordinarily liberating thing to bring into your life is the ability to live with a looser grip on expectations.

- The aim of a vision board is to utterly stimulate your senses to feeling the essence of what you desire.

- As you regularly focus with intent on the images on your vision board, or do creative visualisation meditations, allow yourself to completely trust that your desires will happen. In fact, invoke feelings that they already have!

CHAPTER 11

The Art of Self-Care

Well-ordered self-love is right and natural.

THOMAS AQUINAS

It is vital to take care of yourself while doing this deep and courageous work. As you deal with challenging and life-changing situations and emotions, looking after your mental, emotional and physical health helps you feel good. And when you feel good, you are operating at a higher level and you are of much more benefit to yourself and those around you. Self-care is the constant repetition of small habits, which together will soothe you and ensure you are at your optimum.

It is worth noting that when we make resolutions to care for ourselves better, they can sometimes come from a place of judgement and self-critical thinking. For example, we might decide that we should have a particular body shape, and we give ourselves a very hard time if that is difficult to do within a certain self-imposed time frame – or at all! This thinking can steep us in shame, and keep us stagnant. Also become aware of when you use the word 'should'. It can be a sign that we are being overly hard on ourselves.

True self-care will help you to take your power back, grow in wisdom and understand yourself better and will not involve any harsh judgement of yourself.

Below are self-care routines for your mind, body and spirit. We are all unique, so create a bespoke nourishment plan for yourself from the suggestions provided.

A good start to the day

The choices you make upon waking will have a profound impact on your day. If you hit the ground running, immediately facing into worldly obligations, checking your phone, emails and so on, you will probably feel overwhelmed and stressed.

A good start, on the other hand, will energise and excite you and give you the energy and courage needed to meet the day in a focused and centred way. By getting up a little earlier and creating a practice that suits you, you can set the tone of the day ahead and choose the mood you will use to respond to circumstances. I truly believe that setting up your morning in a good way will utterly change how your day unfolds.

- Wake up with a gentle alarm call rather than a harsh alarm bell that almost gives you a fright on waking! There are many gentle tones available on phone alarms. Allowing yourself one or two snooze presses is a gentler way to wake and allows for greater dream recall. If you can wake naturally, then all the better.

- A morning meditation is a wonderful practice to get yourself ready for the day and to set your intentions. The guided meditations that accompany this book contain a ten-minute morning guided meditation that really gives you a positive start to your day.

- Ten minutes of journaling can also be very useful. Getting your thoughts and concerns down on the page and out of your head will give you clarity.

- Your gratitude journal practice can be a lovely way to start the day.

- Some gentle exercise or yoga in the morning will wake up your body and senses. A morning walk or run in nature also works wonders, if that is possible.

- Eating a healthy breakfast of something that you really enjoy will start your day well. Make it special, almost a ritual. Use beautiful cups, bowls or plates. Honour yourself.

- If you have children, getting them into a routine of getting themselves up and ready for the day will give you more time.

- Make a resolve not to check your emails, social media, news, TV or radio for at least a half an hour after waking.

- Put on some of your favourite upbeat music and boogie in the shower!

- Perhaps you could write the mood you wish to bring in for the day in the steam on the shower door or mirror, for example: Today I move with ease!

If you feel, however, that there is little room for change in your existing routine, try making each activity you engage in upon waking a ritual in its own right. The time you spend every day savouring a soothing cup of tea or washing away tension in a hot shower can serve as a powerful reminder of the need to care for yourself.

It's not all about pampering

Self-care is not all about pampering yourself. At times, self-care is not comfortable or easy. This component of self-care helps you to prevent self-sabotage or procrastination.

Instead of asking yourself, 'What should I do?' ask, 'Who am I being?' Are you being true to the woman you aspire to be? Would she do this?

These particular acts of self-care can be the last thing we feel like doing. It might mean going out for that planned walk or run rather plonking down on the sofa with a glass of wine or a session of Netflix. It might entail seeing a doctor or dentist for a check-up, going for that cervical or breast check that you have been putting off, examining your unfinished business or having that difficult conversation. It can be getting your bank account in order or pinning down a date to have your car serviced. It can be doing that task that has been lurking on your to-do list for an age. These are often not things we relish doing, but they are vital to our self-care.

Healthy boundaries

The novelist Paulo Coelho wisely said, 'When you say yes to others, make sure you are not saying no to yourself.' Recognise that your time, energy and emotional reserves are valuable. Become aware of the people, activities or responsibilities that no longer serve you; we have looked into that in Chapter 7: Overcoming Negative Thinking. It can be hard to say no, especially to those close to you and you may fear rejection if you do. But by establishing healthy boundaries, you nourish both your self-esteem and your relationships. You do things because you want to, not because you feel obliged.

Make a list of things that you no longer want to do. Some examples might be:

- I no longer want to check work emails after 8 p.m.
- I no longer want to attend functions or events because I feel I have to.
- I no longer want to be involved in gossipy conversations.
- I no longer want to be involved in that committee or group.
- I no longer want to say yes to everything I'm asked to do – only to things that feel right.

Decluttering

Taking steps to eliminate physical clutter in your environment, be that your home or your office, has the side effect of soothing your mental and emotional senses. It will help you become unstuck and will allow you to reclaim your power and energise you to move forward into a life you love.

An uncluttered life gives you greater efficiency and effectiveness. You will have a lighter sense of being and that gives you a feeling of freedom where you can become more present, capable and confident. If your environment feels burdened and chaotic it can get in the way of making positive lifestyle changes.

Begin with one space or room, and sort your stuff into three piles:

* **Pile 1** I don't love or need this.
* **Pile 2** I need this.
* **Pile 3** I love this.

Pile 1 are the items to get rid of. Remember, one woman's trash can be another woman's treasure. See if there are things that can be useful to others or donated to a charity shop.

With **Pile 2**, check to see if there are there photos, letters or memories you are holding on to from past relationships or situations. It can be liberating to shed these items and clear the path for new relationships and situations to emerge in your life.

Pile 3 contains the items you keep. However, there may come a time, as you change and evolve, when those things may become part of your second pile or even your third.

Work through your home or work space one area at a time. Trying to do it all at once may be overwhelming.

Think also of decluttering your digital space. Is your inbox overflowing? Unsubscribe from emails that you no longer wish to receive.

Getting a good night's sleep

There's nothing like a good night's rest. If we don't get enough sleep, we become reactive and overly emotional. It is difficult to concentrate and to get tasks done effectively. You know the feeling! Your evening routine is just as important as your morning routine.

- Try to stick to the same wake-up times and bedtimes, even at weekends. This will help regulate your body's clock and can help you fall asleep and stay asleep for the night.

- Limit caffeine, alcohol and nicotine before bedtime as they interfere with your sleep cycle and can have you waking in the middle of the night.

- Avoid large meals at night by making dinnertime earlier in the evening. Steer clear of heavy or rich foods within two hours of bed. Spicy or acidic foods can cause heartburn.

- Avoid drinking too many liquids in the evening as this may result in frequent trips to the loo throughout the night.

- Eating lots of sugar and refined carbohydrates such as white bread, white rice or pasta during the day can cause you to wake at night, pulling you out of deep, restorative stages of sleep.

- Try to exercise every day.

- Keep your phone on silent and resist the urge to check emails or social media for at least an hour before bedtime. TVs and bright screens trick your mind into thinking it is daytime and keep you awake longer.

* Avoid watching or listening to news, anxiety-provoking TV programmes or aggravating social media feeds for at least an hour before sleep.

* If you have trouble sleeping at night, try to avoid napping, especially in the afternoon. Power napping can help you get through the day, but if you find that you can't fall asleep at night, cutting out these naps can help. If, however, you can take power naps during the day without them affecting your night-time sleep, I highly recommend them. They can be a great way of moving from one activity to another, clearing your energy and mind, and giving you clarity and vigour for the next task.

* Take a look at your bedroom. Does it embody the conditions you need for sleep? Your bedroom should be cool; between 15.5 and 19 degrees is the optimal temperature for sleeping well.

* Having your room clear of clutter will soothe your mind. Are the colours of the walls and furniture soothing to you? Blues and greens have been found to be the best colours for a good night's sleep.

* It is good not to have TVs or computers in your bedroom.

* Your bedroom should be free from any light. Consider using blackout curtains, eye shades or ear plugs. Check your room for noises or other distractions.

- Ensure that your mattress and pillows are comfortable and supportive.

- A relaxing, routine activity right before bedtime conducted away from bright lights is a great help. You could take a relaxing candlelit bubble bath or bathe your feet in water with oils. Read a good book or apply a face mask, and enjoy either with a cup of chamomile tea. An evening meditation is also wonderful.

- Essential oils can be a pleasant way to enhance your experience of rest and relaxation. Making essential oils part of your bedtime routine can help train your mind to associate the specific scent with falling asleep. You can dilute essential oils with an air diffuser or, with a base oil, massage a few drops onto a specific part of your body, such as the forehead, neck, chest, wrist, hands, or toes. You can also rub a few drops into your hands and breathe the scents in deeply. If you like, mix the oils with Epsom salts or baking soda and add this to your bedtime bath. Another option is to add a few drops of your chosen essential oil to a pot of boiled water, sit with your face over the pot and a towel over your head to create a tent effect, and breathe in the aromas for a few minutes. There are also face diffusers available that do the same thing. This process can provide relief for sleep apnea or nasal/sinus congestion.

The best oils to help you sleep well are:

- Lavender
- Bergamot
- Valerian
- Ylang Ylang
- Clary Sage
- Sandalwood
- Sweet Marjoram
- Cedarwood
- Chamomile

Meditation

Meditation offers clarity and peace of mind, and gives you time to rest and reflect. If I have been in a stressful situation, the first thing I pull out of my self-care toolkit is meditation. Even five minutes can get you back on an even keel.

The benefits of meditation are undeniable. They include:

* Reducing pain and improvement of the body's immune system.
* Reducing stress.
* Decreasing feelings of depression, anxiety, anger and confusion.
* An increase in blood flow along with a slower heart rate.
* Increased energy and vitality.
* Providing a sense of calm and balance.
* Helping to reverse heart disease.
* Helping to control thoughts and calm the monkey mind.

To accompany this book, I have created seven guided meditations. Most of them are about fifteen to twenty minutes long, except for the morning and evening meditations, which are ten and eight minutes long respectively. They are available on CD or as digital downloads at www.healingcreations.ie.

1) MORNING MEDITATION

When you wake, you can set your intentions for the day by doing this short guided meditation. It will allow you to set intentions as to how you want your day to go. And if things go awry, you are in a much clearer and relaxed place to deal with any adversity.

2) OVERCOMING FEAR MEDITATION

Yes fear, that old chestnut. Fear will keep arising as you move forward on your journey. Fear will always be your companion and getting to know your fear, to talk and reason with it is a powerful practice. In this deep meditation you will meet the imagined embodiment of your fear as a personality and in conversing with it you can let go of your fears one by one.

3) GRATITUDE MEDITATION

This deep gratitude meditation guides you through all of your life and the people, services and things to be grateful for. The attitude of gratitude is such a powerful act. This meditation will give you the experience of completely embodying the emotion of gratitude. You will feel it in every cell and emanating from your very being. Watch the magic happen afterwards, as the external world reacts to the gratitude you have given it.

4) FORGIVENESS MEDITATION

Forgiveness is a key attribute to a successful and stress-free life. The wonderful Maya Angelou said, 'It's one of the greatest gifts you can give yourself, to forgive. Forgive everybody.' This meditation brings you on a peaceful journey to meet a person you wish to forgive. It is a powerful practice and is best done by forgiving one person in each meditation. Forgive first the person who has hurt you least, working your way up to the person who has hurt you most.

5) CREATIVE VISUALISATION MEDITATION

This meditation takes you to a particular day three years into the future. You will project yourself into your future life and really embody how it feels. You visualise every aspect of this future self and literally are this person on this day three years from now.

6) EVENING MEDITATION

At night-time, by meditating to clear away the stresses of the day, you set yourself up for a great night's sleep. You can leave behind worries and anxieties and instead of percolating the negative in your mind while you sleep, you can percolate the positive!

7) DEEP SLEEP MEDITATION WITH BODY SCAN

This meditation is designed for those nights when you just can't seem to nod off. It is a relaxing and clearing meditation that includes a deep body scan, rotating your consciousness around the body.

The music chosen to accompany the meditations has been created with healing intentions focused on specific frequencies that have proven useful in facilitating a certain mood, feeling, or brainwave state, giving you a powerful meditation experience.

Summary

- Self-care is the constant repetition of small habits, which together will soothe you and ensure you are at your optimum.

- Self-care habits and routines include:
  - Creating a good start to the day. By getting up a little earlier and creating a practice that suits you, you can set the tone and mood of the day ahead.
  - Addressing tasks and jobs you may have been putting off, like going to the dentist, getting your car serviced or making appointments for medical check-ups.
  - Maintaining healthy boundaries, where you nourish both your self-esteem and your relationships. You do things because you want to, not because you feel obliged.
  - Decluttering your home or office. When you do this you will have a lighter sense of being and that gives you a feeling of freedom where you can become more present, capable and confident.
  - Getting a good night's sleep. The suggestions include establishing a relaxing environment, avoidance of too much food or drink before bedtime, and turning off communication devices an hour before retiring.
  - Meditation. This is a powerful and invaluable aid to clarity and peace of mind, and also gives you time to rest and reflect.

Endnote

Congratulations on beginning the brave journey to find your own authentic path in the world. Be assured that the journey is worth it. If you move forward with good intentions, no matter if nothing seems to change for a while, things *will* change. Your path will reveal itself to you, sometimes with ease and at other times in more challenging ways.

Becoming your true self may take some time, especially when you may have been used to behaving in a particular way, like being a people pleaser or keeping your opinions to yourself. Take as long as you need to develop and grow. I believe the journey of personal transformation is lifelong, and there is no limit as to how much we can grow and achieve.

You may be surprised at sudden flashes of clarity as you develop and shed unwanted habits. Enjoy these moments – indeed, celebrate them! You may have already experienced some positive changes. This is only the beginning, because as you continue implementing what you have learned, the changes will happen faster and more magically. You are on a path of growth that will not stop.

Addressing and working through difficult situations will serve as invaluable lessons for the future, and as you look back, you will see how you have gradually accrued self-awareness and peace of mind along the way. 'I have sent you nothing but angels' is a beautiful quote from Neale Donald Walsch's book, *The Little Soul and the Sun*. This means that every person and every situation you encounter holds within them a valuable jewel of wisdom for you to place in your pocket to give you sustenance on your path.

It is only as time passes that you will notice how less reactive you have become, and that it is much harder to press your buttons. You will also feel lighter and find humour in so many more things, and your mind will be more open to inspiration and creativity.

Take the time to sit down once in a while to assess how you are dealing with particular situations. Compare your current progress with the previous few months, and give yourself credit for the positive changes that you have accomplished and how far you have travelled.

Finally, know that through all your hard work and effort, you will ultimately be rewarded by becoming the incredible and wonderful woman you were always meant to be.

Patricia Fitzgerald